# What I Learned
# Before I Sold
# to Warren Buffett

1/27/04

Mike –

A little bird
told me to send
this out!
Thanks for
coming to Colo!

# What I Learned Before I Sold to Warren Buffett

## An Entrepreneur's Guide to Developing a Highly Successful Company

**Barnett C. Helzberg, Jr.**

**WILEY**

John Wiley & Sons, Inc.

Published by John Wiley & Sons, Inc., Hoboken, New Jersey.
Published simultaneously in Canada.

For general information on our other products and services, or technical support,
please contact our Customer Care Department within the United States at
800-762-2974, outside the United States at 317-572-3993 or fax 317-572-4002.

Wiley also publishes its books in a variety of electronic formats. Some content that
appears in print may not be available in electronic books.

For more information about Wiley products, visit our web site at www.wiley.com.

ISBN 0-471-27114-4

Printed in the United States of America

10  9  8  7  6  5  4  3  2

*This book is dedicated to my favorite journalist and Mom, Gladys Feld Helzberg (1905–1973), who gave her sons so very much in every way, including love of the language and empathy for others.*

*And to Dad, B. C. Helzberg, Sr. (1903–1976), who gave me so many of the teachings that are in this book as well as so many thoughts on how to be a happy and successful person.*

# Acknowledgments

Thanks to my bride, Shirley Bush Helzberg, who gives me strength, spirit, and inspiration daily, Warren Buffett for his help and encouragement, David Pugh, my patient and inspirational editor, Sam Fleishman, my wonderful and conscientious agent, Patricia Brown Glenn, for her vital advice, Kim Isenhower, who claims she redid this book eighty times, Paul Wenske, without whom it would not have happened, and to those who contributed by editing, adding material, and encouraging me, including Dr. Bob Clark, Dr. Alice Ginott Cohn, Ted Cohn, Dr. Rich Davis, Senator Bob Dole, Tom Eblen, Pola Firestone, Tom Gill, John Goodman, Bar Helzberg, Bush Helzberg, Charles Helzberg, Rabbi Morris Margolies, Harvey Mackay, John McMeel, Dick Miller, Eric Morgenstern, Shanny Morgenstern, Dr. Pierre Mornell, Eleanor Mundis, Joanna Pomeranz (of PV&M), Beth Smith, Dr. Harvey Thomas, E.J. Waters, and the friends, students, Helzberg Diamonds Associates, Helzberg Entrepreneurial Mentoring Program members, and my mentors, who put up with me and taught me through the years.

# Contents

# A Confession of Plagiarism

Plagiarism has become an exciting and controversial subject with the press and some renowned authors lately. I was always taught that many, many people were out there developing ideas I could use. I have found that to be true throughout my life. These thoughts and ideas have all been borrowed or stolen from many wise people, therefore this confession.

I have always solicited other's opinions and tried to listen intently when they were espousing things, even when I was in pretty violent disagreement. Therefore, I claim only one original idea in my entire life, and with this book, wish only to reveal myself as a plagiarist of wonderful ideas from a lot of great people through the years.

Think of the world as your garden of marvelous people and ideas with unlimited picking rights for you. Enjoy the flowers!

# Selling to the
# World's Best Investor

(OR HOW TO PITCH YOUR COMPANY TO THE BEST INVESTOR
IN THE WORLD IN 30 SECONDS OR LESS)

As I walked past the Plaza Hotel near 58th Street and Fifth Avenue on a glorious May morning in 1994, I heard someone call out, "Warren Buffett!" Turning in the direction of the voice, I saw a woman in a bright red dress stop Buffett on the sidewalk and start a friendly conversation with him. Buffett, dressed comfortably in an off-the-rack suit, listened patiently to the woman, who, it turned out, was a shareholder of Berkshire Hathaway, Buffett's hugely successful company. At the time, the legendary investor was the second richest man in the United States, and a share of Berkshire stock was about $20,000.

As it happened, I was in New York that day to meet with our financial advisors at Morgan Stanley to talk about our company, which at the time operated 143 jewelry stores nationwide (more than 245 now). Personally, I felt uncomfortable expanding the company beyond my ability to know every store manager on a first-name basis. We had grown well beyond that point, and we were still growing. We had no interest in going public. We didn't want to be pressured to pay more attention to quarterly earnings and stock price than to the long-term operational health of the company and the well-being of our associates. We certainly didn't want some financial butcher carving up this jewel and selling it piecemeal. I also didn't want my associates spitting on my grave.

As the woman said her goodbyes and turned to go, and as Buffett prepared to cross the street, I saw my own opportunity, stepped forward and thrust out my hand. "Hello, Mr. Buffett," I said. "I'm Barnett Helzberg of Helzberg Diamonds in Kansas City." I didn't sense any recognition in his face, but he politely shook my hand and said "Hello" back, willing, if not eager, to hear me out.

Then, right there on the sidewalk, as busy New Yorkers rushed past us and street traffic buzzed around us, I told one of the most astute businessmen in America why he ought to consider buying our family's 79-year-old jewelry business, headquartered in North Kansas City, Missouri. "I believe that our company matches your criteria for investment," I said. To which he replied, simply, "Send me the information. It will be confidential."

My conversation with Buffett lasted no more than half a minute. (In fact, the account of my sidewalk pitch to Buffett was featured in the January 2002 issue of *Harvard Management Communication Letter* as an example of the classic elevator pitch, which entails selling your idea in the time it takes to ride an elevator three stories.) My idea, of course, was to grab his attention. How often do you encounter Warren Buffett on a sidewalk and pique his curiosity in your family company?

As I walked away, however, I wondered whether my approach might have seemed abrupt, if not downright presumptuous. Yet, I felt certain that our successful, three-generation family business made a perfect fit with Buffett's Berkshire Hathaway, which *Fortune* magazine has repeatedly named as one of the 10 most respected companies in America. In 1994, Berkshire's $11.9 billion net worth was greater than Coca-Cola and Pepsico combined. It was a collection of 30 businesses including such signature names as See's Candy, World Book, and Nebraska Furniture Mart. It was the largest shareholder in Gillette, Coca-Cola, and the American Express Company.

To be sure, if you're looking for a gauge to measure how well your company has grown and developed, and how well your management has led and cared for your company's associates, you can't do any better than to find yourself in a situation where Warren Buffett wants to buy it. And that's just the situation in which we found ourselves in 1994.

Imagine our gut-busting pride when, as the third-generation owners of Helzberg, Buffett later explained why he decided to buy our business: "We associate ourselves with some real jewels of the American business world. And I think it's quite fitting that Helzberg joins this collection of jewels. It's just exactly the kind of company we like to invest in. It's got outstanding management. It's got a leadership position. It's on the move. I would hate to compete with you fellows. I'd rather be on your side of the fence. And that's the side we're going to be on."

My dream buyer for the family business all along was Warren Buffett. I knew we could trust him to keep the headquarters in Kansas City, resist changing the company's character, and retain the jobs of all of Helzberg's associates. It might have been simpler to sell to the highest bidder, but that notion seemed as sensible as choosing a brain surgeon based on the lowest price rather than on talent and reputation.

I had purchased four shares of Berkshire Hathaway stock in 1989 just so I could attend Berkshire's annual meetings and pick up some of Buffett's wisdom. His presentations are warm and unpretentious. He genuinely enjoys people. He's often quoted saying, "Great people do great things." He also likes to say, "We only buy companies that we trust." That certainly proved to be true when he bought Helzberg Diamonds.

My first visit to a Berkshire Hathaway annual meeting was quite a revelation and taught me a great deal about Warren Buffett and his philosophies. My notes included, "Hire seven footers, that is, hire people with incredible abilities." Another very, very strong impression was obtained through an answer he gave a Kellogg Business School student who asked, "How do I determine which job to take?" Warren's answer was simply, "Get a job you love, at a company you respect!" His people orientation was obvious and since I had been taught from day one by my Dad that "Business *is* people," this was most impressive.

Buffett recounted the story of how he acquired our company to shareholders this way: "Barnett said he had a business we might be interested in. When people say that, it usually turns out they have a lemonade stand with potential, of course, to quickly grow into the next Microsoft. So I simply asked Barnett to send me particulars. That, I thought to myself, will be the end of that."

In fact, it did almost end there. I promptly went home and sent Buffett nothing, afflicted with hang-ups about confidentiality. I'm the kind of guy who asks for someone's Social Security number before I tell them the time. But one night I reread the chairman's letter in the Berkshire annual report. There was Buffett again inviting companies that meet his acquisition criteria to send him information, and he would "promise complete confidentiality." While shaving the next morning, I looked at the slow learner in the mirror and began to scold myself for procrastinating. "He told you in person it would be confidential. He told you in writing. Do you want it set to music? Send him the information." So I finally did.

Not long after we sent Buffett our financial information, he called us up and told us he wanted to talk. He said we were a lot like Berkshire, which to me was the ultimate compliment. Soon we were in his office in Omaha negotiating a sale.

His incredible diplomacy was strongly evident during our visit. Our CPA from Deloitte & Touche told him the incredibly high price that we had come up with for the business, based on what he had paid for another company. I recall he had no reaction even though it was actually about double the price that he ultimately paid. I am sure Mr. Buffett and I both thought it was ridiculously high!

"This can be the fastest deal in history," Buffett said. "But what about due diligence?" I asked, surprised at how fast the negotiations were moving. Most suitors demand to see every scrap of paper you've ever generated and to interview every top manager. That wasn't Buffett's way. "I can smell these things," Buffett said. "This one smells good."

That would not be my last surprise. I asked about a non-compete clause. "You'll certainly want that, won't you?" I asked. Buffett shrugged. "You wouldn't do anything to hurt this company," he said. When a guy says that to you, he has you on your honor for the rest of your life.

When Buffett buys a company, he's not looking for a quick resale to make a buck. He told us, "Someone asked one time what my favorite holding period for securities is and I said forever. And that's exactly the way we feel about our businesses."

When we were ready to leave his office and asked if a cab could be called, he insisted on walking us to the elevator, riding it down with us, and standing on the street to wait with us for the cab. Typical Buffett treatment! Our poor cab driver was desperate to know what company we were with. I finally fibbed and said we were with a hardware retailer.

Warren Buffett's approach to purchasing companies is very straightforward. He will give an answer immediately if he has any interest, and he will immediately give you a non-negotiable price.

A close friend whose company he bought was told by his attorney that there are seven things the attorney puts in every acquisition contract on behalf of a client who is to be acquired. When Berkshire purchased my friend's business, he requested none of these because they were already in the contract. That tells one a great deal about the character of Warren Buffett. His is a vitally important role model in the landscape of American business, proving that nice guys can finish first (or second after Bill Gates!).

After buying Helzberg, Buffett explained to his shareholders that "our ownership structure enables sellers to know that when I say we are buying to keep, the promise means something. For our part," he continued, "we like dealing with owners who care what happens to their companies and people. A buyer is likely to find fewer unpleasant surprises dealing with that type of seller than with one simply auctioning off his business."

Easy to say, but Buffett makes it work. How? By buying companies with smart and intuitive leaders and then staying out of their way. When he bought us, Buffett's empire of 22,000 associates was overseen by only 11 people at his Omaha head-quarters. No micromanagement there. And talk about trust. Explaining how he makes this hands-off approach work, Buffett said that it was "because the managers operate with total autonomy and they do such a terrific job we really don't need anyone to supervise them. Managers run their own shows. They don't have to report to central management," he said. "When we get somebody who is a .400 hitter we don't start telling them how to swing."

True to his word, Buffett didn't change a hair in the leader-ship of Helzberg. He was happy with the company's leadership under Jeff Comment, formerly president of Wanamaker's. "Jeff was our kind of manager," Buffett would later say, adding, "In fact, we would not have bought the business if Jeff had not been there to run it. Buying a retailer without good management is like buying the Eiffel Tower without an elevator."

Buffett's purchase of Helzberg Diamonds validated the pain-staking efforts by our family, along with so many wonderful associates, to build a national operation of profitable customer-focused jewelry stores second to none for providing quality, value, and service. The national recognition of our efforts was flattering. In a November 1994 industry report, Goldman Sachs called Helzberg Diamonds the "Nordstrom of the Jewelry Business."

The report noted that Helzberg's average per-store sales of more than $1.7 million in 1994 was nearly double the industry average. Goldman Sachs said Helzberg set the standard of excellence for other jewelers in its market niche, selling to middle- and upper-middle-class consumers. The report concluded that just as other department stores have had to learn to compete with Nordstrom, so other credit jewelry companies will develop strategies to compete effectively with Helzberg.

Berkshire was then one of about a dozen companies in the United States that had a AAA rating from Standard and Poor's. Buffett told us after our negotiations, "You are associated with a company that is really regarded as one of the bluest of blue chips. And in associating with Helzberg's we know we have joined with another company that, in its own field, is comparably regarded." I couldn't think of a more gracious thing to say.

I think if my Dad, Barnett Sr., and grandfather, Morris, had still been alive, they too would feel proud and comfortable that our family business, which started in 1915 from a single store in Kansas City, Kansas, and had grown by 1994 into a group of 143 stores in 23 states, with total sales of $282 million, was in capable hands. As Buffett himself finally described the deal that began on a New York sidewalk, "We weren't talking lemonade stands."

---

### Mining for Diamonds

♦ Dad told us that the higher you go, the nicer they get. Mr. Buffett exemplifies that rule.

♦ Consider using fair contracts rather than one where the other party thinks you are playing "gotcha." Berkshire does.

♦ Class and business success are not mutually exclusive.

♦ For a priceless educational opportunity buy one share of Berkshire Hathaway B stock so after you get the annual report (available on the web to all), you can go to the annual meeting (for shareholders only). Some claim that one Berkshire meeting is more valuable than a semester-long MBA class.

# Know Thyself: What It Takes
## to Be an Entrepreneur

My father was 14 when he took over the family business. My grandfather, Morris Helzberg, had a stroke and there was no one else to run the little jewelry shop in Kansas City, Kansas. His brother Morton was in dental school and another brother, Gilbert, was headed to World War I duty. Because Dad was in school, the family persuaded an uncle to watch the store each day until Dad arrived from school. I don't believe my father ever questioned the family's decision.

The evidence indicates he took to the task naturally, with true entrepreneurial drive. He was a born salesman, regularly staying at the shop past closing time just to help one more customer. His teacher became concerned that the focus was shifting from school to work and one day demanded, "Barnett, where do you study your lessons?" Dad innocently replied, "On the street car," to the great amusement of his classmates.

At 17, Dad moved the business into a larger, grander building and with the high spirits of youth proclaimed himself a diamond merchant. The shop sold the same mix of rings and watches as everyone else, but the label let the world know he had big plans for himself and the family business. During the Depression he became a symbol of courage and positive thinking for the embattled community when he doubled the size of our Kansas City, Missouri, store in 1932. He nurtured and demanded that same positive drive to succeed, whatever the challenges, in his three sons.

Dad gave me summertime employment when I was 15. I wasn't sure what to expect. A timid and obedient child, I only asked Dad not to make me sell anything. Fat chance. Dad knew the importance of learning by doing, so of course, I started by selling. My love for it began after the exhilaration of my first sale (which I think was a radio), and I took rejections in stride. I was smitten with the customer interaction and the ensuing relationship that resulted.

Modest as that first sale was, I began to have confidence that I could do this. It wasn't work, it was fun. At the end of the summer I placed in the top 10 in a companywide watch sales contest. I had not yet earned the right to sell diamonds. I was an entrepreneur, master of my own destiny. I could do whatever I set my mind to. Anything was possible. I can't tell you where other entrepreneurs get their drive, but I'll bet many catch the bug young like I did.

The feeling that you are your own boss, that your future is in your hands, is a frightening and thrilling prospect. I became president of Helzberg Diamonds in 1962 at age 29, when my father became ill and asked me to take over. I was nervous and definitely not ready, but I did so with absolute backing from Dad and the entire family. It wasn't always smooth, but it was always interesting. I made mistakes and had my share of failures, but my enthusiasm and the backing of my family never wavered.

All successful people have failures. How many times did you fall before you could walk? I'm told Babe Ruth struck out 1330 times, but he's remembered for hitting 714 home runs. Despite missteps, entrepreneurs are a special breed who do not give up on the larger goals.

The late Ewing Kauffman (a mentor of mine), founder of Marion Laboratories and former owner of The Kansas City Royals baseball team, became a pharmaceutical salesman in the 1950s and turned his love for people into a phenomenal success. He beat every quota and earned more than the boss. The next year the boss reduced his territory. Up to the challenge, Kauffman sold even more, again earning more than the boss. The next year, his boss cut his commission. By then, Kauffman had had enough. He quit and started his own pharmaceutical business, packaging his own products in his basement and selling them from the trunk of his car. In 1989, Kauffman sold Marion Labs to Merrell Dow for $6.5 billion.

Not everyone wants to become a Ewing Kauffman, though some will. I see young entrepreneurs everyday in our Helzberg Entrepreneurial Mentoring Program (a program for less experienced entrepreneurs to be matched up with more experienced entrepreneurs) who have similar dreams and drive: people who prefer to take their futures into their own hands. No one has an easy prescription to become a successful entrepreneur. If they say they do, they're fibbing. It takes a lot of luck, which often translates into seeing and seizing opportunities before someone else does.

Entrepreneurs come in every shape, size, gender, and socioeconomic background. Some were entrepreneurs from the moment they opened their first lemonade stand. Others became entrepreneurs out of necessity: they got laid off or fired, or they fired their boss and got out of a bad situation. Downsizing creates armies of new entrepreneurs.

Entrepreneurs are driven to succeed. They possess an almost naive belief that nothing can stand in their way, they are mentally deaf to those who belittle their chances, they love to compete, and they have the skills of broken field runners who take the bumps and bruises along the way, change course when necessary, and stay focused on the goal.

If this is not you, don't try to fool yourself. It's not worth it. Thinking you can start your own business or wanting to be your own boss, just because you hate your job, when you really have no desire or stamina to go it on your own, is courting disaster. Where there is no real will, there is no way.

Some aren't willing to pay the price of giving up some time with their families. The choice is far from obvious, but to some there is no choice when something grabs them by the nape of the neck and drags them into the ring.

According to government statistics, about a million businesses start each year, and more than half fail within the first two years because of poor financing, lack of management discipline, and/or entrepreneurial skills. Some people are more enamored by the concept than the reality. They would rather contemplate the beauty of the mountain from the base.

The entrepreneur wants to climb the mountain first, briefly appreciate the gorgeous vistas from the summit, and then find the next mountain. If you possess this obsession of seeing your own creative notions succeed and are willing to pay the price, whether starting your own business or expanding and improving an existing one, then you have no choice but to pursue the life of an entrepreneur. My own particular motivation included an obsession with proving wrong the "shirtsleeves to shirtsleeves in three generations" myth.

More than 22 million small businesses already exist in America. They account for 99 percent of all American businesses. They employ 53 percent of the private workforce and contribute over half of the nation's private gross domestic product. All that goes to show entrepreneurs are successful every day, and they provide real benefits to their community and nation.

You can be a success if you want it badly enough. Today's prospective entrepreneurs are far more thoughtful than many of my generation. Those I have contact with seem to have a mature grasp of the need to know their strengths and weaknesses and to measure the plusses and minuses before they plunge into a venture. They think carefully about the price to be paid in family time and working hours.

There is no magic formula or litmus test; you just need to realize the depth of the commitment. However, you can draw general conclusions about successful entrepreneurs:

- *Decisive:* They rely on intuition, street smarts, and even gut feel. They can catch on to big ideas without having to go through the logic and details that slow others down.
- *Risk-takers:* They calculate odds but at the same time are quick to "get off the dime." If action carries downside risks, it comes at a price they are willing to pay.
- *Persistent:* Failure is written off as down payment against the success they believe will come if they simply keep at it. They always have a plan B, if not X, Y, or Z.

- *Tough-minded:* They may dream of big breakthroughs, but they live in the real world when it comes to keeping score on results. They need to know what works in order to refigure the odds for the next trial run.
- *Independent:* They prefer to march to their own drumbeat, often turning out to be harder on themselves than any boss.
- *Money-sensitive:* "Cash in the till" is one clear message that whatever they tried worked out poorly or well. The best of them understand that profit is opinion but cash is fact.
- *Never satisfied:* As fast as they get wherever they've been trying to go, they come up with a new set of itches to replace the old ones. They are perpetually "just getting started" no matter how successful they become.
- *Passionate:* They love what they are doing. Time moves quickly for them. They are exempt from boredom.

In addition to the characteristics listed above, successful entrepreneurs tend to have a certain set of competencies on an emotional level. They:

- Like being the leader.
- Enjoy being the boss.
- Take criticism and rejection well.
- Want to know how they can improve to be successful.
- Know their strengths and weaknesses.
- Know when and where they need help.
- Know the wisdom of hiring people with strengths in their own areas of weakness.
- Don't let criticisms or setbacks get in the way of relationships.
- Are willing to work for the most demanding, unreasonable boss ever (themselves).
- Are willing to work hard, exhibiting the discipline necessary to make a success.
- Are willing to pay the very high price of lost time with family.

- Are willing initially to make smaller earnings (hopefully for a limited time).

At the bottom line, entrepreneurs fashion their ideas into a business. They:

- *Differentiate:* They know how to make an idea stand out from others in the marketplace.
- *Live finance:* They understand the need to find sufficient funding to grow and maintain the business.
- *Execute:* They use a combination of skills, guts, and luck to bring everything together and make it work.

Entrepreneurs may not be all that easy to live with when it comes to patience or teamwork. They aren't likely to spend much time figuring out how to win friends. They can be workaholics. It can be easy to misread them as impractical dreamers, even con artists. Yet, in the final analysis they are the ones capable of providing jobs, security, and income for others on the lookout for a spot from which to participate in the American dream. Without entrepreneurs, the business scene becomes bland and repetitive, so that even the bureaucrats find themselves wishing for someone with the courage and smarts to make something interesting happen.

Even so, you don't have to start a business in order to be an entrepreneur. I certainly did not. Some people inherit small businesses or are thrust into leadership in them like I was. Others run entrepreneurial departments within larger enterprises. The ideas in this book will help those entrepreneurs, too. If you decide after reading this that this is not the life for you, then you also have received timely advice.

After all this, do you still want to be an entrepreneur? I hope so. If so, I support and salute you. My own business experience has taught me that it can be the greatest job in the world. Sure, there will be bumps, but then as Yogi reminded us, "It ain't over till it's over." And the ecstasies have a way of overbalancing the agonies. That's what Dad would tell you, and as we all know, "Father knows best."

# Part I

# Managing

# 1 Concerning Yourself with Only the Controllables

*When growing up, I was intrigued that my father only concerned himself with those business elements that were controllable. He refused to acknowledge the Depression and did quite well during that period. He was unwilling to talk about recessions or 20-inch snowfalls. He only thought about and talked about those conditions within his control.*

*I saw this daily in Dad's actions. I never knew when the country was in a recession because Dad wouldn't talk about it. People would suggest we close the store on Labor Day because everyone would be out of town. He'd say, "How many will be gone?" Of course, we'd stay open and do just fine.*

*Dad was a great believer in "not sweating the small stuff." He taught us to concern ourselves only with those things over which we have* control. *I thought he was unique in this until I realized this is one of the key common traits of highly successful people. Those folks* are never victims; *they take what comes and handle the situation. The rest is a waste of time.*

I have chosen Pogo the Possum, the clever creation of cartoonist Walt Kelly, as my patron saint. Pogo said, "We have met the enemy and they is us." This philosophy allows little room for blaming others, but it can certainly lead to success. James Carville, Democratic campaign strategist in 1992, also agrees with Pogo: "That's the smartest thing said in the history of man," he noted several years ago, as quoted in a *Time* magazine article.

The "deal only with the controllables" philosophy helps you focus your attention where it ought to be. Keeping this principle in mind helps save time and resources. After all, if you can't do anything about a problem, just move on.

---

### Mining for Diamonds

♦ Deal only with controllables.
♦ Never be a victim.
♦ Paint yourself in a corner with one choice—to be successful.

---

*You cannot always control circumstances, but you can control your own thoughts.*                  —Charles Popplestown

*Worry is interest on money never borrowed.*        —Anonymous

# 2 Making Your Business Different

*The most understandable measure of value in diamonds is size. Everyone understands that a 1-carat diamond is bigger than a ½-carat diamond, so that is the consumer's basic orientation. Amazingly, Dad approached this marketing situation 180° differently then nearly every other jeweler in the United States. (As you read this, please keep in mind that our customers at that time were folks of very moderate incomes.)*

*His concept was that he refused to sell a diamond solitaire in an engagement ring that was not "perfect," that is, internally flawless, with good color, good cut, and absolute clarity. As he struggled for a name for this concept, he picked up a box of baking soda on which he read, "This baking soda is certified to be perfect." Thus, Helzberg "Certified Perfect" Diamonds.*

*The result was that when the customer entered our store, the diamonds were actually smaller for the money. We explained to them that they were absolutely perfect and were the finest money could buy, and we felt that as a symbol of love they owed this to their bride.*

What did this do? First and foremost in my own heart, I believe the biggest thing it did was create pride within our associates at every level of the company, knowing that we had a totally unique stance and refused to sell any other quality in diamond solitaires. It showed tremendous respect for customers who weren't used to being treated that way.

It also created a unique selling proposition at Helzberg Diamonds and made us dramatically different. It gave us the opportunity to tell our customer across the counter, "You don't have to buy at Helzberg's, but we strongly suggest you get a perfect diamond." Since virtually nobody else carried them for most of those years, this was a wonderful and unique reason for the customer to shop at Helzberg Diamonds. We created our own market. Rather than being in the diamond market, we created the perfect diamond market. Far larger than the Helzberg Certified Perfect Diamond concept was the kind of tone it set in the organization. I feel this was probably the greatest single strategy decision Dad ever made.

Years later when it became nearly impossible to get Certified Perfect quality in certain stones, I went to him with a number of reasons to change our policy. I pointed out to him that we had not been able to buy a Certified Perfect marquise diamond for a two-year period, and the fact that our business was grading up and many of these customers wanted larger stones for the money. Because of my good reasons and undoubtedly in great part because I was his son, he blessed the plan. As it turned out this decision was fortuitous; in addition to the reasons I'd given him that day, Certified Perfect Diamonds became virtually extinct in many markets of the world diamond trade.

Some other unique and unusual techniques Dad used were:

1. He set a policy absolutely refusing to negotiate prices on merchandise (though not unique, it was highly unusual).
2. Further, he demanded we treat all customers with respect and that, in many cases, created an unparalleled loyalty. I can actually remember a customer who came in and begged me to order him a television set, although we didn't sell televisions, because he did not want to open an account at any other store.
3. Another idea, which many people have never forgotten to this very day, was the "Teenage Watch Club." The

advertising told teenagers that they could come in with parent's permission and purchase any watch up to $50 and establish their own credit without anyone else signing for them. The ads stated, "There is nothing legally binding in this procedure!" We always secured the parent's permission and made many friends this way. To illustrate the power of this concept, the policeman who stopped my brother for speeding said to him, "How could I give a ticket to someone who gave me my very first chance to establish credit?" Generally, credit is based on where you have had credit, and this creates a catch-22 situation for most folks since there seems to be no way to get credit unless you have credit references! Who do you think these young folks thought of first a few years later when engagement time came? Many years later I started to realize how very powerful that particular concept was. As in many people's experience, the older you get, the smarter your parents get!

### Mining for Diamonds

♦ Find ways to separate yourself from the competition. Show a clear, definable difference.
♦ Principles build your business, not the profit motive.
♦ Entrepreneurs should always be massaging a successful formula in looking for ways to improve and to be up-to-date in building differences from the competition.
♦ If you are in a crowded, competitive market, create your own market, that is, not the diamond market, the perfect diamond market; not the beef market; the angus beef market; not the beer market; the freshest beer market.
♦ Be different—and better! You need a unique selling proposition.
♦ Remember the tremendous benefits to spirit and morale when you operate with principles your associates can be especially proud of.

*Bigger is not better . . . better is better*
—Vivien Jennings, Rainy Day Books,
a community bookstore, Fairway, Kansas

# 3 Highest and Best Use of Your Time

*When you are operating a group of retail stores, there is always the usual bell curve of weak to great performing stores. At one point we were struggling with a store doing $800,000 in volume and through gargantuan efforts trying to get to $850,000 in annual sales. Much conventional practice dictates committing great effort to the weakest segment. When I discussed this with my friend Steve Lieberman of Minneapolis, the hot dog magnate who ran hundreds of Carousel Snack Bars in shopping centers for many years, he said, "You make more money closing bad stores than opening new ones."*

*His philosophy made sense. We decided we would rather spend time and effort on a $4.5 million store that could ultimately achieve annual sales of $6 million than on a lower-volume store with less potential. Did this mean we gave up immediately when things did not work? Absolutely not; if the store lacked great people, proper merchandising, or other controllable variables, by all means we fixed it. However, our attitude became to upgrade the herd annually, closing the weakest stores each year.*

Each activity you undertake exacts the price of not being able to pursue alternative activities (sometimes called *opportunity cost*). You are investing the time and talents of your associates. What is the actual cost of sending a highly talented person to create an average performance out of a dry well

9

rather than sending him or her to a gusher that can be turned into a super-gusher? The cost is far more than the cost of that individual. Thus, the cost of putting out fires where problems exist and putting fingers in dikes where leaks exist is extremely high in the sense of decreased progress or missed opportunities. Peter Drucker calls that "feeding the problems and starving the opportunities." The temptation is to devote oneself to fixing the problems that cry out for fixing, but feeding the opportunities can be so much more profitable. The question, "Is what I am doing bringing me closer to my objective?" should be restated as, "Is what I am doing bringing me closer to my objective than an alternate activity that I could be doing?"

Because of their semipermanency and their unlimited parasitic appetite, underperforming operations destroy the good people you send there for turnaround while simultaneously depriving those great managers and great teammates of an exciting opportunity as well as putting capital to nonproductive uses. Management's challenge is to take advantage of the unlimited opportunity to focus the talents of its most talented people on winners. Riding the winners to success was what created the large average sales volume of the Helzberg Diamonds stores. Perhaps one of the key reasons Warren Buffett has been the world's most successful investor—he does not buy turnaround opportunities, only successful companies.

Concentrating on winners will help maximize your profits and make your life a whole lot more fun. What greater excitement than riding those winners to the finish line and getting that garland of roses? It sure beats moving poor performers up to mediocre.

Focus is your lever to success. As the leader you need to be sure you and your team are doing the right things, and as managers they need to be doing things right. Doing the right things is the leadership component—that is clearly up to you. The doing things right component is the province of the managers to whom you have delegated the responsibility. *Anything* that decreases focus on these right things inhibits progress. Investing unlimited effort in failing projects does not create success.

Do not underestimate the incredible amount of mental discipline it takes to focus yourself and your teammates. Wonderful alternatives and seductive opportunities abound and temptations to go in multiple directions are unlimited. Of course, consistently working on the basics can get boring, especially when things are going well. Why not open a print shop or sign shop, do your own payroll, or engage in a myriad of services to save money? Such temptations take you away from the constant improvement needed in your core business to be the best in your industry.

Commit yourself to be the best, define what that means, and focus on the head of that pin like no one in your industry. Have a clear simple objective, let your team develop the roadmap, and go for it!

---

### Mining for Diamonds

♦ Are you focusing on your core business, where you are best?
♦ Are you *eliminating* activities that decrease your focus?
♦ Are you focusing on the *fewest,* most powerful opportunities?
♦ Less is truly more when you are committed to the right "less."
♦ To win, focus on achievers—the right people matched with top opportunities.

---

*Less is more.*          —Le Corbusier (1887–1965), Swiss architect

# 4 Super Service: Friend to the Entrepreneur

*After purchasing my new car, I was going through the material that came with it. The message on the instructional cassette tape was, "You should never take your car through an automatic car wash," and in the handbook it stated, "You can take your car through an automatic car wash." I called the auto dealers's service department to ask which was correct—the cassette tape or the handbook. The serviceman responded, "Please bring your car in because we would prefer to wash it for you at no charge!"*

*Arriving at the dealership, I discovered that from 8:30 A.M. to 3:30 P.M., six days a week, the company washes customers' cars at no charge whatsoever. I was hoping it would have a waiting room where one could read and buy a Diet Coca-Cola. I found not only a waiting room, but free Diet Cokes! When I asked if there was a phone I could use, I was told there were two. One phone offered was in a private office.*

The company offered exceptional service. Yes, they bought my soul offering free car washes and free Diet Coke. This tripled my enjoyment of my car. In the past I went to the dealership only when the car needed service or to look at a new car. Rare and not always pleasant! With the additional services they saw me a lot more often and in a far brighter mood. I am looking forward to my next auto purchase—and will certainly shop there.

*That same day I went to the grocery store to get a few items. Unloading the groceries, I found that the home phone numbers of the owners, Mike and Libby, were listed right on the sack with the invitation to call if I was not happy with the store. In addition to the signs they had around the store about making me a happy customer, they proved they meant it. It was clear that the owners took responsibility for good service.*

Although I had no reason to call the owners about the grocery store service, the information and statement on the sack certainly made me believe that they cared.

*Al and Nancy acquired their TCBY yogurt franchise on May 15, 1996. By summer 2002, the volume had virtually doubled. Long lines of customers patiently wait to be served. Why did the business double in the same location and with the same merchandise and no particular local economic miracles?*

*Here are Nancy's thoughts: "It comes down to serving the customer, giving them full attention, not posting hours and staying open later if people are still coming in, putting up a community bulletin board, which of course includes pictures of Emma, our first grandchild, helping seniors to read the menus, instructing our staff to memorize five names a week (tell the customer your name and ask theirs, explaining that you are working to memorize five names per week—'If I forget when you come back I will give you a free topping'), family involvement with our son, Jess, and his wife running the store sometimes. There is lots of training that goes on with staff so they know our expectations."*

*They build relationships—my cousin George called me telling me Nancy gave him the news about my grandson-to-be before I could. There is always a cheery greeting and a question like "How is your school doing?"*

*Nancy and Al have turned down some offers of*
*multiple locations, preferring to build a small gold mine*
*rather than a large silver mine. They may consider a sec-*
*ond store in the future. I'll bet Jess and his wife will run*
*one or the other. You can bet that as a steady customer,*
*I sure hope Al and Nancy don't leave me!*

Great service exists—fortunately for entrepreneurs it's a rarity.
What an opportunity for the ambitious until super-service
becomes commonplace (it never will). Remember super service
is in the eye of the beholder—and it need not be expensive.
Remembering the customer's name and the customer's needs
and just showing an attitude of wanting to help rather than
just selling the customer can build the loyalty you are looking
for. How about a nice handwritten note out of the blue thanking them for paying promptly or just thanking them for their
business?

At Helzberg Diamonds we were happy to clean rings in our
ultrasonic machines for our visitors and replace watch batteries
free. The actual doing of these things is not really the point. I
always said "to know our people is to love them." The way
these services are rendered makes the difference, not the service itself. I prefer bad food and good service to good food and
bad service. (For a great book of horror stories and success stories about customer service, you'll enjoy *WAYMISH . . . Why*
*Are You Making It So Hard . . . for me to give you my money?*
by Ted Cohn and Ray Considine.)

You can provide outstanding service—and own your customer. It will make everyone's job more fun. It will build your
business. Great entrepreneurs recognize the goal is the total customer experience, not just the quality and price of goods or
services purchased or given. Now for the key question: How do
you get it done in your organization?

You need to give positive reinforcement to those who
render great service to the customer. At Helzberg Diamonds I
sent personal hand-written notes to the folks who got great cus-

tomer comments thanking them, and those notes found their way to the bulletin boards and stayed up quite a while. When I went to get my auto repaired, the service representative who introduced himself told me the factory would be writing me regarding his service quality. When I picked up my car, the manager had a note on the invoice that if any of my grades of the service were under 5 to let him know.

The other side of the coin is that you must jump very quickly on the wrong kind of customer service and promote a three-strikes-and-you're-out mentality and never accept less than the best in customer treatment from your staff. That must be built in as one of the absolutes of your business culture. The quality of customer service is not negotiable.

---

### Mining for Diamonds

♦ Bad service at your competitors provides unlimited opportunity for you. Cash in.
♦ Exceed your customers' expectations (underpromise—overdeliver).
♦ Make building loyalty (long-term customer value), not just satisfaction, your prime goal.
♦ Reward and reinforce good customer service.
♦ Use a three-strikes-and-you're-out policy on employee retention when poor customer service is rendered.

---

### MAX'S LAWS©

1. This restaurant is run for the enjoyment and pleasure of our customers not the convenience of the staff or the owners.
2. You get a free round of drinks if any one of our staff comes up and says, "*Is everything all right?*" When we ask questions, they'll be good ones.

3. You must get your mustard and ketchup before your burger, sandwich or fries.

4. We hate soggy fries. If yours aren't crisp, the way you like them—send them back—maybe the kitchen will get the message.

5. Corned beef and pastrami are good because they contain some fat; however, with today's dietary consciousness, our corned beef and pastrami are now extra lean. So ask for a little fat for that traditional taste. If you want something with no fat, how about our turkey or turkey pastrami?

6. The turkey is always fresh. Period.

7. Our iced tea is table brewed. Just pour it over a big glass of ice.

8. You'll love our breads and pastries. They are made fresh daily in Max's Bakery and Kitchen.

9. Warning: We bake our own sourdough crusty as can be. If you like soft bread, eat the middle.

10. Our ice cream sauces are a point of pride. They're made in New York by a certified chocoholic who refuses therapy. They are simply the best in the country. And we don't boast idly.

11. We bring ice cream sauces from New York City. Eat here. Save the airfare.

12. This is a bad place for a diet and a good place for a diet.

13. Our desserts are excessive because nothing succeeds like excess. We encourage sharing if you're not super hungry.

14. Substitutions are okay by us; don't be bashful, you've got a mouth, use it.

15. We use cholesterol-free oil for frying and sautéing; anything can be grilled fat-free.

16. If you are a single diner and are greeted with the expression, "*Just one?*", dinner is on us.

17. We agree that the customer is always right. If there is a problem with your food or service, call for the manager—we'll fix it in a flash. But, if you finish your plate—it couldn't have been all that bad! Now, could it?

Menu from Max's Opera Cafe® of Palo Alto. © 1985 Max's World Inc.

**5 Keeping Customers**

*When fundraising for my alma mater for the University of Michigan Business School Annual Fund, I wrote a number of people and asked why they had discontinued annual giving. Their answer—the only time I hear from you is when you want money! That was not the University's perception. They thought the expensive, very professionally done publications were showing their givers how valid their help was, but perception of the giver is the reality.*

*I learned more about keeping customers when I had breakfast with my college roommate, Howard Boasberg, who after college moved from Buffalo, New York, to Kansas City. Howard was a tremendous success in the public relations business! After breakfast I understood that a lot of Howard's success was due to "walking around in the other person's moccasins." Howard related to me that most companies go to their clients on an annual basis with a written questionnaire about the quality of services. He indicated he did this regularly on an eyeball-to-eyeball basis.*

*Further, he indicated that he carefully told people well in advance exactly what everything was going to cost them. He pointed out that most divorces in professional relationships happen because of communication shortcomings rather than quality of work. He felt that was avoidable.*

Having been a client of lots of professional organizations, I certainly subscribe to his philosophies. As a consumer of professional services, don't you deserve this treatment? Don't your customers? How often do you contact them to build a bond and learn more about their dissatisfactions? How can you improve your service to them?

This applies to your internal customers—your employees or associates. They need to be convinced of the quality, pride, and rightness of the behaviors of your organization. They are important because everything flows from them. Do the actual behaviors of the company (not just mission and vision statements) make them proud they work there? Asking if your associates would be proud of any action will help you make better decisions. Is this a place you would be proud to work?

---

### Mining for Diamonds

♦ Don't wait until dissatisfaction arises to "make love to" your customer! Take the temperature of your relationship on a regular personal basis!

♦ Invest in your present customers. Don't focus on new business to the exclusion of those feeding you!

♦ Keep selling your employees and associates by your actions, just as you should with your customers.

---

*To be successful, have your heart in your business, and your business in your heart.*
                                    —Thomas Watson (1914–1993), IBM President

# 6 Your Complaining Customers: Your Greatest Opportunity

*A man was driving down the highway on a sweltering summer day when one of the tires on his car suddenly blew out. Stopping to search his trunk, he was relieved to find a spare tire but frustrated that he didn't find a jack. So he started hiking to the nearest gas station, more than a mile back down the road.*

*As he walked along, drenched in sweat, he began to think perhaps the station attendant might not want to lend him a jack. After all, he already had a spare tire, and he wasn't planning to have the flat repaired right away. The station attendant really didn't have anything to gain by helping him. The farther the man walked, the hotter and angrier he became, directing all his discomfort at the station attendant, who he was now convinced would surely refuse to lend him a jack.*

*By the time he got to the gas station, the man was so steamed about the attendant refusing to lend him a jack on this miserable, hot day that he grabbed the startled gas station attendant by his shoulders and demanded: "Why won't you lend me that jack?"*

At Helzberg Diamonds, we called this The Jack Story, and we used it to illustrate a key customer service challenge: the angry and suspicious customer. So many consumers have been mistreated that by the time they get to you, they already anticipate mediocre to terrible service. They may feel awkward asking for help or be so certain their needs will be ignored that they can be defensive and even combative. But they also pose great opportunities to nurture strong relationships that transform unhappy critics into loyal customers and boosters.

In fact, I firmly believe the best customers you may ever have will be the ones who came to you angry but were disarmed by your willingness to listen and to respond sympathetically to their complaints. They leave feeling special because you went out of your way to help resolve their problems. These are the customers who return again and again because they know you care about them and want them to be happy.

I remember a woman who marched into Helzberg Diamonds in Des Moines, Iowa, carrying a broken piece of Melmac dinnerware. We sold thousands of sets of Melmac at $29.95 each, along with a lifetime guarantee against breakage. Despite the guarantee, the customer's demeanor made it clear she believed the store would look for a way to weasel out of replacing the item.

Instead, our store manager, L.W. Montgomery, listened attentively as the woman expressed her displeasure, putting her at ease. He then told her how sorry he was that she was inconvenienced and, without another word, rushed into a storage room and produced a replacement. The woman was so pleased with this unconditional effort to retain her as a loyal customer that she lingered in the store and bought a watch. Perhaps she needed the watch, but she wouldn't have had to buy it at Helzberg's. She certainly wasn't in the mood to buy a watch when she steamed into our store. The lesson? Provide prompt and courteous service and you will win over customers for life.

Later, I jokingly suggested to Mr. Montgomery that maybe we should put an extra piece of broken Melmac in every box of dinnerware we sold. Then, we would have other chances to prove we stood behind our Helzberg guarantees. Of course, we wouldn't really do that. But the point is to find every opportunity to show your customers you want to take care of them. Rather than be reluctant about resolving a customer's problem, do it with joy. Thank your customer for taking the time and trouble to complain. Dad always said, "If you're going to take care of the customer anyway, why not get the benefit?"

How right he was. A recent *Wall Street Journal* article explained the incredible value of making the angry customer happy compared with the value of the loyal customer. The point: loyalty is far more valuable than mere satisfaction. The FedEx concept of calculating the lifetime value of loyalty (that is, $20,000 per year × 20 years is a $400,000 customer) dramatically portrays the concept. Be proud of the fact that unhappy customers think enough of you to express their unhappiness. The biggest losses to your business are the customers who never come back to complain about a perceived problem. Instead, they tell all their friends that they'll "never deal with that lousy company again."

One study I read estimates that one unhappy customer tells 18 other people about a bad experience. What a huge missed opportunity. I much prefer that formerly unhappy customers tell their friends how we fixed their problems. The unhappy customer who tells you he or she is unhappy is a treasure to be coddled and potentially far more valuable than the satisfied customer. Consider spreading this feeling among your associates so they can consider the unhappy customer a real opportunity rather than a problem to be solved.

---

### Mining for Diamonds

- Always realize the need to empathize with your customers. Use The Jack Story to illustrate this to your associates.
- Embrace unhappy customers, who have the potential to become your loyal (not just satisfied) boosters.
- Satisfy and rectify with a smile! If you're going to take care of them anyway, why not get the benefit?

---

*The object is not to satisfy the customer but to delight the customer.*
—Anonymous

**7 Managing Risk**

When the company started expanding to neighborhood
shopping districts right after World War II, many said it
did not make sense, but Dad saw that our competition
hadn't really tapped the markets. In some markets,
what passed for jewelry stores were glorified watch-
making shops. Helzberg Diamonds went in with full-
line jewelry stores, many of which turned out to be
highly successful.

Among my own forays, I got the company into the
mail-order hearing-aid business. This related (or so I
thought) to a successful mail-order division we were
operating at the time. Somehow, I came up with the idea
of using mailing lists of older people and offering them
a hearing aid for $29.95. The venture was a sure win-
ner, very predictable, a numbers game of simply antici-
pating the percentage of orders we'd get from the
solicitations we sent out. What was not anticipated is
that hearing aids are a very individual item, like trying
on shoes. We sold 40,000 hearing aids at $29.95. Over
two-thirds came back because they didn't work for
everyone.

What I did learn was that by being a little calmer
and more mature we could have sold a few hundred and
waited to see the whole story. A test includes the whole
cycle, including waiting for all the returns. Of course, I
failed to hear Dad when he repeatedly said, "A lot of
these are coming back," after he passed the shipping dock

*daily. I guess I predated the"dot.com" phenomenon—*
*fortunately the whole world did not know!*

*The failed venture didn't affect our core jewelry*
*business and we were able to exercise an option to*
*return unsold hearing aids to the manufacturer. We had*
*negotiated that option up front as a way to reduce the*
*risk to us of going into a brand new business—one we*
*clearly didn't understand. What could have been a dis-*
*aster for us turned out to be far less damaging because*
*of the safety net we had from the option to return*
*unsold merchandise.*

*Successful companies learn to manage risks. The*
*risk that I might fall doesn't stop me from skiing, how-*
*ever. I love to ski, despite (and possibly to some extent*
*because of) the risks.*

In retail, a new store always involves risk. However, there
were ways we could minimize it. If a jeweler was doing $2
million per year in the mall, we knew there was business to be
had if we opened in that mall. To further reduce the risks of
making mistakes in pricing, advertising, or merchandising, we
studied the market extensively. But at the end of the day, we
found that our key success factor was people. We believed in
our people. We felt they knew how to operate a store better
than anyone in the business, so we decreased the risks inherent
in reaching into a new market by transferring in proven managers and associates from successful stores.

We were careful to assess risks in terms of several criteria.
What is the amount of risk we can take at the present time?
How important is the opportunity? Are we betting the farm or
just the lower 40 acres? Levels of risk vary with the magnitude
of the effort. On occasion all of us in business misjudge the
chances for success of a particular effort. Develop the absolute
worst case scenario and see if you can handle it financially and

emotionally; leave a margin of safety for the unpredictable—
recessions, floods, fires, droughts, and September 11.

A level of pretesting can also mitigate the risk of a new venture. For example, when we wanted to test a new radical idea, we learned to test it first. Then we could focus on correcting and fine tuning the procedures. "Fail small and succeed big" became my mantra at some too late date! The new idea always involves adjustments. Grow the idea *after* debugging. When possible, toe-dipping is the way to go in starting new ventures.

You also can minimize your risks by thoroughly studying your market. You can learn a lot from your competitors' successes. You cannot always judge your potential for success by the lack of success of others. If someone else isn't making money in a particular market, it doesn't mean that you can't. Perhaps your competitors simply haven't done a good job of exploring all the possibilities of the market.

Oddly, with the advent of the covered malls we (the third-generation Helzbergs) went to sleep and were very late into the game. We nearly destroyed the company by our tardiness but were lucky enough, with tremendous effort, to recover the fumble and run it to the end zone.

We finally realized that we could be successful and manage the risks. We had one mall-based jewelry store in Overland Park, Kansas, a suburb of Kansas City, and sales at that store were growing stronger all the time. We had first-rate management and service-oriented sales associates, and we knew how to price merchandise attractively. So we forged ahead with multiple mall locations in our markets. In Cinderella City Shopping Center in the Denver area we learned that an unknown jeweler could do business in a new market with a great team and a good location.

Our reward was huge, resulting in virtually unlimited growth opportunities for the company. Our average sales per store grew in volume to more than $2 million by the time we sold the company in 1995. At the time we had grown to 143 stores, mostly mall-based.

## Mining for Diamonds

♦ You can't avoid risk. You can minimize risk by weighing the worst possible outcome against the potential for rewards.
♦ You are always taking risk, whether changing or not changing.
♦ Carefully think of ways to reduce your risk when you are entering into a new venture.
♦ Sticking with the business you know reduces risk.
♦ Remember, you don't know what you don't know.
♦ Your biggest risk may be not taking one.

*Take calculated risks. That is quite different from being rash.*
—George S. Patton (1885–1945), general, war hero

*You miss all the shots you never take.*
—Wayne Gretzky, professional hockey player

# 8 Should Incentives Be Based on Profit or Volume?

*One of the worst plans I ever instituted was having managers act as owners by rewarding them purely on a profit basis. This plan ultimately backfired because some store managers became excessively concerned with overhead rather than sales. One manager worried about cutting the light bill; others focused on inventory, keeping it extremely low because of charges for carrying costs. Profit as the only yardstick gave managers incentive to concentrate on some of the wrong things and misfocused their efforts!*

*This changed in 1970 when Martin Ross joined the company as executive vice president. He teamed with Ron Atcheson, our vice president for operations. That wise and extraordinarily talented team decided the corporate office should control payroll and expenses and let the store managers concentrate only on sales, sales, and sales. That did it! The stores focused only on sales, which drove average volume ever higher, helping the company grow in a major way.*

Understanding the importance of profit *and* sales volume in business was one of the hardest concepts for me to fully comprehend. Thankfully, I was fortunate enough to work with people who knew the importance of balancing each.

What about executive management? Should profit be the be-all and end-all for them? Absolutely not! After 39 years of learning in business, I see my associates' tremendous wisdom in deciding bonuses should be based on both sales volume *and* net profit. No one should be working on a pure profit bonus. *It encourages short-term thinking.* Therefore, we created bonuses based partly on profit and partly on volume.

*Profits are short-run* and *volume is long-run.* If your sales volume is climbing (and you are not "giving the merchandise or services away"), then you've either added customers or are making better customers out of your present ones or doing both. The increase has everything to do with your customers' buying decisions. It means you and your associates are doing a better job. Your customers are voting! Growing sales are vital to your company's future.

Profit is certainly a necessity. However, profit alone can be a dangerous measurement and can lead to decisions that don't pay off in the long run. Balance between both is key!

---

### Mining for Diamonds

♦ Profit is short-run. It is the *byproduct* of a job well done.
♦ Sales volume is long-run. Building growing, *profitable* sales volume in existing entities (stores, factories, etc.) is paramount to success (in retail this is called a *same store sales increase*).
♦ Focus on sales or both profit and sales, depending on who is receiving the incentive and their level of control on sales or profits.

---

*Balance—the ultimate goal.*

—Ricky Lankford

# 9 Consultants: Bane or Bargain?

*Erwin, a brilliant consultant and CPA, visited Helzberg's and for a princely sum for those days ($100 a day) looked at our operations and made suggestions. Because of the quality of his suggestions, we invited him for a second visit, but when the bill came this time it was for $300! I called him and said, "Erwin, I don't understand this bill!" His reply was, "You didn't do any of the things I talked to you about during my first visit." (I got my whipping!).*

*Erwin made his point. There was no use spending our money and his time if we weren't going to move on any of his suggestions. He was no more anxious to waste our money than we were.*

The old story about consultants borrowing your watch, telling you the time, and then keeping your watch can be valid. Consultants should be checked out like any other hire of equal importance. We sometimes found outsiders could bring something to the party, but the key is implementation. If your team is resentful and not receptive or if no timetable and follow-up on new ideas or procedures are set up, you will be wasting precious time and money.

What is the right way to bring in a consultant? Plant the seeds well in advance that you may want to get some outside help on a particular area of the business—on a one-to-one basis with those most involved. They are closer than you are to the problems, dealing with them on a daily basis. They can best define the challenge. To get the greatest benefit, including ideas your own team will bring up that may be even better, discuss in depth the suggestions made by the consultant and the implementation of them. Put in more agony, get more ecstacy!

A good deal of this also applies to your paid and unpaid advisors, whether they are friends or mentors. Their time is precious and if you don't really value their thoughts, why waste their time as well as your own? Time is your most valuable asset. The bank will give you more money back at the end of the year if you put it in a certificate of deposit but your time cannot be increased.

## Mining for Diamonds

♦ Remember Erwin! Don't use time or money if you don't plan to move on some suggestions!

♦ Analyze each idea separately, talking each through with others. The ideas may stimulate other or better ideas from the group.

♦ Be action-oriented. List what steps are to be taken, who is responsible, and milestone and completion dates. Review progress at regular meetings with the group in attendance.

♦ If the attitude of your insiders is resentment, jealousy, or anger, do not waste your time on consultants. You need team backing.

♦ The biggest danger is an interested attitude on the part of your team and no progress. You need babies, not labor pains! The weekly or monthly follow-up and progress report is an absolute necessity.

*Change is a door that can only be opened from the inside.*
*—Terry Neil*

**10** Keeping Your Ego in Check

*"Barnett, whenever you go out of town, everything around here runs great," my colleagues used to kid me. Sure they said it tongue-in-cheek; at least I think so. But I took it as a compliment. Knowing of my lack of immortality, I have always felt if I did my job right, my disappearance would not harm the company. I believe that has been proven as Helzberg Diamonds has continued to grow and has achieved new profit records since we sold to Berkshire Hathaway.*

*If you can say that if you fell dead tomorrow, your company would prosper quite nicely without you, it's a sign that you have been a good leader. When I sold to Warren Buffett, I felt sure that Helzberg Diamonds would just keep getting better. It didn't need me to succeed. That's one of the reasons Buffett bought us. And after he did, he didn't make one change in the management.*

A tremendous amount of research went into the excellent Jim Collins book *Good to Great*. One of the surprising revelations about the companies that went from good to great was the humility of so many of the leaders. In many cases they are not the charismatic celebrity leaders you might expect. Most are names you would not even recognize.

Many large companies falter because their leaders never establish a succession plan. But small companies and entrepreneurial ventures also can take this lesson to heart. If the soul of the company is wrapped around the entrepreneur, its long-term survival is questionable. In fact, entrepreneurs who put their own ego before the company's welfare aren't thinking about the people who are left behind, who helped build the company and have a stake in its future. Leaders who believe their companies would go to seed without them ought to be boiled in oil. I think it's more a feather in your cap if you can brag the business will keep growing long after you're gone because of all the talented people you hired who don't need you to tell them what to do next.

Just because your name is on the door of a corner office doesn't mean you have a corner on the truth. A lot of so-called business gurus preach that ego is good—that "it ain't braggin' if you done it." I'm sorry, I don't buy it. It is counterproductive, and a false sense of bravado. People who have a healthy confidence in their abilities don't have to flaunt their egos.

Ego simply gets in the way. One of the more perplexing and unfortunate manifestations of success is the inability to handle it. In fact, success can be far more difficult to handle than failure. I know, I've experienced both. (For the record, I still prefer success, even with all its challenges.)

One unfortunate side effect can be a growing inability to listen to others and a belief in the permanent correctness of whatever you have started in motion. It's as if there is an invisible fungus that grows over the ears of some successful business people that tragically blocks their ability to listen. People with out-of-control egos often can't stand to have other smart people around. So they lose those people, and are the worse for it.

I love the thought that God gave us Mozart to keep us all humble. I've been blessed with many opportunities to remain humble and I do believe being the dumbest guy in the room can be the smartest thing you can do as a leader. I've never kidded myself. Our business really began to perk when I hired people smarter than me. Often, all I had to do was get out of their way. When you find these great people, they make your dreams come true, and then they go beyond your dreams. If you don't care who gets the credit, you can get anything done.

---

### Mining for Diamonds

♦ A dangerous side effect of success can be a growing inability to listen to the valuable advice of others.

♦ Ego can create a barrier between you and the smart people you need to help you build success.

♦ If you don't care who gets the credit, you can make your dreams come true.

---

*The Wicked Leader is he who the people despise.*
*The Good Leader is he who the people revere.*
*The Great Leader is he who the people say, "We did it ourselves."*
—Lao Tsu (c. 604–c. 531 B.C.E.), Chinese Taoist philosopher

*Big people grow, little people swell.*          —B. C. Helzberg, Sr.

# 11 Setting Specific Measurable Goals

*One day in 1970 while visiting our store in Oklahoma City's Crossroads Mall, Jim Fisher, the store manager, asked me to step outside with him. When we were alone, he asked me not to mention to his staff that we had set a monthly sales goal of $20,000 for his store. At first I was puzzled. Jim was one of our best managers. Surely, a $20,000 monthly goal was within his capabilities.*

*Jim must have sensed my surprise, for he broke into a smile. Then he explained, to my delight, that not only was $20,000 not a problem, but he and his Oklahoma City associates had set their own monthly sales goal at $40,000, twice the company's goal. His team hit $38,000 in sales, 90 percent above anything the general office had expected of Jim and his energetic sales staff. Talk about setting high expectations for yourself and your associates.*

Jim's experience underscored for me the power of setting high but realistic goals. If you set your expectations high enough, you are reaching for the stars. You may just hit the moon! Goals allow you to budget your time, set deadlines, establish priorities, and assign responsibilities. Tangible goals also give you the ability to measure your performance. For instance, members of Jim's sales team knew exactly what was expected, right down to dollars of sales needed per hour by each individual. The expectations were clear, attainable, and measurable.

The goal wasn't just to improve sales, it was to make $40,000 in sales.

Setting individual goals encourages associates to take active roles in making the company successful. Making goals measurable allows you to reward associates and celebrate their successes. Another great lesson I learned from Jim is that 9 times out of 10 your associates will set their own goals higher than those you would set for them.

Here are a few other things to remember about goals:

- They have to be tangible and realistic.
- They have to be measurable.
- They have to be met by a deadline.
- They have to be communicated clearly to everyone.
- They should be rewarded when they are met or exceeded.
- They should be limited in number (not more than three to achieve a bonus) so that focus can be maintained.

---

### Mining for Diamonds

◆ Set your goals high! Reach for the stars! (You may just hit the moon!)
◆ Goals allow you to measure how far you've come.
◆ Never, never tell anyone to do their best. Give specific expectations.

---

*The person who makes a success of living is the one who sees his goal steadily and aims for it unswervingly.*
  —Cecil B. De Mille (1881–1959), film director and producer

**12 Believing in People**

*Early in the growth of our company, we began imple-
menting rules, believing this was a good way to avoid
recurrence of misdirected actions. When something
went wrong or someone screwed up, we added another
rule. It got to the point where the main thing growing
was the list of rules. Associates were afraid to act on
their own for fear they'd make a mistake, but they were
so nervous they made mistakes anyway. Finally, someone pointed out that all these rules were building up this
ugly scar tissue of policies that discouraged people
rather than encouraged them.*

*We saw the light. Although we retained strong ex-
pectations for our stores and for our associates, we
threw out meaningless rules that prevented the self-
starters from applying their own talents and resource-
fulness to meet, and more often exceed, expectations.
We realized that the people who worked for us must be
talented, or why else would we have hired them? Why
not believe in their abilities to make things happen?*

*Rather than fearing they would make mistakes, our
associates began to express to us that they felt trusted
when they made many of their own decisions. We made
sure we recognized their efforts so that they knew someone was aware of their triumphs, because, in truth, if you
don't provide positive feedback for their efforts, many of
your associates will eventually be thinking, "Oh, what's
the use?" Recognition can be as simple as telling sales
people they handled that customer in a caring manner.*

The rich reward for you is that when your associates are motivated to stretch their abilities and contribute to the success of the organization, they will inspire you to accomplish even more, too. It's a variation of the adage, treat others the way you wish to be treated.

If this all sounds Pollyannaish, know there will be disappointments, sometimes you just have to grit your teeth. But if you believe in people, you will on occasion, depending on the risk and the reward, willingly allow them to fail. If someone else's idea isn't as good as yours, but it's still okay, you're often better off allowing it done his or her way. Quality of execution is far more important than the idea.

In order to succeed in an increasingly complex business world, entrepreneurs need the talents of everyone in the organization. Believe in the abilities of others and let them grow and perform at their best. Helping others harvest their triumphs will allow you to achieve more success than you could hope for by insisting everything be done your way. On those inevitable occasions when your faith in an individual is disappointed, take a deep breath. Believe me, many others will delight you by exceeding all expectations.

A basic need of every human being is to feel appreciated. That means more than just being understood, which is important, too. What I'm talking about is being valued for who you are, what you stand for, and what you do to make things better.

Your clients and suppliers want to know that you value their relationships. Your customers want to know that you care about them. Most of all, your associates want to know that you believe their talents contribute to the success of the organization. But to be able to show appreciation, you have to believe in people. An abiding belief in people is essential to your mental health as well as the health of your business.

If you are afraid your suppliers are ripping you off, you might approach them with suspicion. If you think your customers are taking advantage of you, you might treat them like trespassers. If you think your employees are cheating you, you

might micromanage their every move. Pursue this negative behavior long enough and there's a good chance you'll become
paralyzed with a galloping case of paranoia, and bring the
progress of the organization to a grinding and painful halt.

### Mining for Diamonds

♦ Individuals need to be appreciated. Think of how you or your
business expresses appreciation as a key part of your responsibility.

♦ Don't overemphasize rules. Consider fostering a culture that
shows belief in the ability of the individual to take the right
action.

♦ Don't be deterred by rare experiences when your belief in
someone results in disappointment.

♦ Bitterness will be highly counterproductive to your future
success. Follow the divorced man who said, "I am not bitter.
I will not pay that price."

### THE CRITERIA OF EMOTIONAL MATURITY

*The ability to deal constructively with reality*

*The capacity to adapt to change*

*A relative freedom from symptoms that are produced by
tensions & anxieties*

*The capacity to find more satisfaction in giving than receiving*

*The capacity to relate to other people in a consistent manner
with mutual satisfaction & helpfulness*

*The capacity to sublimate, to direct one's instinctive hostile
energy into creative & constructive outlets*

*The capacity to love*

> —William C. Menninger, MD (1899–1966), co-founder,
> The Menniger Foundation

# 13 Never Burn a Bridge

*Jim (not his real name), a potential landlord, was a rather rotund fellow, and as he stared out the window and loudly enjoyed his popcorn, we, an unknown company, pitched him on the amazing benefits to his shopping centers if he would put a Helzberg Diamonds in them. We were unable to break his fascination with his popcorn and apparently some tree visible from the window.*

*After we left the suite where his company was promoting and leasing their centers, we agreed to continue to follow Dad's maxim: Never burn a bridge with anyone even if they treat you like a fencepost. We would theorize that next week he would be our most important landlord and we would be working together.*

*This is one of the most valuable lessons Dad gave us and we never had reason to regret treating people like they wanted to be treated—and that sometimes included not treating them like they treated us! This policy can save you lots of regrets and probably lots of time wasted in thinking about what your reaction should be.*

*Like all rules, this has an exception. If your customer is abusing your associate consider very nicely and softly telling them that you cannot serve them properly.*

---

### Mining for Diamonds

- ◆ Treat everyone as they want to be treated.
- ◆ Disregard their treatment of you or your associates.
- ◆ Build the story in your mind that they will be terribly important to you in the future.
- ◆ Exception: If a customer is abusing your associate in the extreme, weigh the possibility of firing the customer. I did it once in 39 years.

---

*You can always give them hell in the morning.*
> —Tom Murphy, former boss of CapCities/ABC,
> as quoted by Warren Buffett

*In real life the most practical advice for leaders is not to treat pawns like pawns, nor princes like princes, but all persons like persons.*
> —James MacGregor Burns, author, historian,
> 1970 Pulitzer Prize winner

**14** **Planning for Disaster**

*One bitterly cold January 11th in the mid 1960s, our executive vice president, J. B. Grossman, my brother Charles, and I went to the First National Bank of Kansas City to make our routine loan. We needed to cover the checks, sent the day before, to our suppliers for the immense amount of merchandise we had bought for the Christmas season. We had a longstanding relationship with First National going back about 30 years.*

*We had gotten the usual letter reassuring us that a $500,000 line of credit was available to us when, as, and if needed. We hardly noticed the last paragraph of the letter which would rescind the bank's obligation if our creditworthiness changed.*

To our shock and surprise, the bank refused to loan us the money! One particular director of the bank felt we were not creditworthy.

After getting over the shock of this situation, we immediately drove to Security National Bank in Kansas City, Kansas, where the Briedenthal family had served Dad for untold years. Morris Briedenthal, Jr. did have one question for us, "How much do you want?" It seemed a matter of seconds for us to obtain the money to back up those checks in flight at that very moment.

We probably did not deserve the loan. In fact, I heard that Mr. Briedenthal, Sr. told his board, "Their Dad learned how to make money and those boys will learn how too."

The risk that day was ruining our reputation and credit rating in the industry. We came to the precipice and were saved

41

by the two-supplier principle. When at death's door, you may be saved by a relationship. We were.

The Security National Bank never lost a penny doing business with Helzberg Diamonds; their friendship never waivered and you can imagine our loyalty.

Did we continue to do business with both banks? Yes, absolutely. Never burn a bridge was our mantra. And we still wanted two suppliers.

When there is no urgency is the time to concern yourself with two suppliers for critical matters. Plants burn, suppliers go bankrupt, floods, earthquakes, and tornadoes occur . . . as well as mergers and sellouts that change the landscape radically. Going to a second source when you are desperate, and the service or product you need is in short supply, will not work. Any good supplier will take care of his own customers before adding new business.

---

### Mining for Diamonds

- Having more than one supplier for each critical need provides you with options and security.
- Building personal relationships with suppliers when appropriate can save your bacon at crunch time.
- Different suppliers have different strengths and weaknesses; why not let them complement each other, fill in for each other's weak areas.
- Get second sources now, when you do not need them.

---

*The best preparation for tomorrow is to do today's work superbly well.*          —Sir William Osler (1849–1919), leading 19th century physician, teacher, and historian

*Go oft to the house of thy friend, for weeds choke the unused path.*
          —Ralph Waldo Emerson (1803–1882),
          author, poet, philosopher

# 15 Turnaround Time at Helzberg Diamonds

A number of years ago, Peter Drucker wrote a fantastic column for The Wall Street Journal about cure-alls in business. Cutting costs and redoubling present efforts, he wrote, wouldn't necessarily cure your business problems. If the world no longer wants to buy buggy whips, cutting payrolls and a layer of middle management is not going to create long-term success. Although these steps may increase short-term profits, they are just Band-Aids for what really ails the company. If you stall the real cure, you may hasten your company's demise (we did stall and almost "demised").

At Helzberg Diamonds, the 60's were tough years with declining volumes and profits. We became addicted to promotions like free tea sets with a purchase —like heroin it started out as a rare promotion and finally we did these costly events monthly. Our customer became educated and waited for the promotion—we were trying to make a dead horse work and he refused. We finally quit these events cold turkey but though that helped, no miracle ensued.

Then in a fit of desperation, we entered the licensed department business operating jewelry departments in discount stores.

We actually compounded Mr. Drucker's felony— first trying to revive the dead downtown stores, then taking the wrong turn for Act II.

Ultimately, and just in time we found our fit with the malls and closed 38 out of the 39 locations including stores and leased departments—moving virtually exclusively to malls.

Life, of course, is never that simple. The two giants of the business, Zale Jewelers and Gordon Jewelers, were going into nearly every mall being built with either one or two stores; they each operated higher-end divisions as well as their basic stores. With far more understanding and foresight than yours truly, they built tremendous loyalty with the developers of the malls. Their leases enabled developers to borrow on them to build the projects. I could only respect this and, at the time, I just said that I hoped someday we would be in that position with the landlords ourselves.

On a cab ride from the airport to the hotel in New York at an early International Council of Shopping Centers convention, I shared a cab with a Kansas City developer, Paul Copaken. I asked for his definition of a good tenant. Of course his definition included the payment of more rent. Since all mall rents are based on the higher of a dollar minimum or a percentage of sales, the higher the sales, the more rent for the landlord. If our store could do $1 million in the same footage as the competitor who did $500,000, our rent would be $50,000 and his $25,000; rents were then generally 5 percent of sales. If the minimum guaranteed rent was $15,000, we would both be paying overage rents—ours would be far more profitable to the property owner. (These numbers date back to 1967.)

Our goal became: "to be the highest dollar volume per square foot jeweler in each mall." This made us interesting to the landlords and we finally got some credibility as a good tenant.

## Mining for Diamonds

♦ Decide where you want to go, and then map the course.
♦ Don't let short-term thinking get in the way of long-term progress.
♦ Plan for long-run success, not short-run profits.
♦ Treat the illness, not the symptoms.

*Flops are part of life's menu, and I'm never a girl to miss out on a course.*
    —Rosalind Russell (1907–1976), actress of stage and screen

# 16 Testing New Ideas: Stacking Your Deck for Success

*In the 1970s, Marty Ross, one of our most innovative executives ever, wanted to get rid of our long-established but increasingly cumbersome practice of financing our own receivables. The industry had handled its own credit for years, and skeptics didn't believe a jeweler could survive without extending in-house credit to customers.*

*Because Marty, one of the early leaders of what is now called Circuit City, came out of the appliance industry, he wasn't influenced by the skeptics. Even so, the stakes were high in terms of loss of interest income and fees from the outside providers of credit. So Marty chose one of our best store managers to test his idea that jewelry stores could make more money if they focused on selling diamonds and left the credit business and interest income to banks and other lenders who were experts in such things.*

*Now, you have to know that the manager Marty chose, Cecil Williamson, who managed our store in the Blue Ridge Mall in Kansas City, could make anything work. You could set diamonds upside down and Cecil could still sell them. But that was the point. Marty wanted his test to succeed, and with Cecil as the manager of the initial test, they fine-tuned the procedures to make the policy work. In fact, it worked very well. Cecil's success rippled through the company, as Marty showed other managers what worked and what didn't. This type of testing and evangelizing became central to our success,*

*and became one of the reasons we were able to move
quickly in the marketplace.*

*After our test of outsourcing customer credit, we
could now say to other Helzberg stores, "it has proved
to be successful." As each of our stores began to imple-
ment the new system, our total focus on buying and selling diamonds, and not on being in the banking business,
brought incalculable dividends. Today, companies like
General Electric and other "private label" credit sources
are providing credit for many prestigious and successful
retailers.*

At one time I believed the best way to evaluate whether a
new product or concept would work in one of our stores
was to simply test the idea in an average store with an average
staff. My simplistic and erroneous thinking was that if the great
new idea could be made to work in an average store, it could
work in all of our stores.

Then I learned a better way, one that made a big difference
for our company, although perhaps it wasn't exactly the business school method. What I learned was that winning entrepreneurs build success into the way they test new ideas or products
by having their best people take on the challenge. Doing everything you can to try to ensure success is a different way to
test. You are, in effect, setting a standard for accomplishment
everyone else can learn from and emulate. Can we make it to
the moon? Not by sending average astronauts. No way. You
send up your best astronauts and prove getting to the moon can
be done.

Many business people are taught that when you test products or ideas, you have to set up a situation that eliminates factors that could bias the results. They're taught they should have
a test group and a control group for comparison, and that they
should control as many variables as possible to get a true com-

parison. These guidelines are great for folks who need scientifically valid results and have time to wait for them. In practice, however, sometimes you have to take intelligent shortcuts in order to get a winning idea to market. It might not work for your business, but it allowed us to test products and ideas quickly and, at the same time, get excellent feedback. If the new idea was implemented first by our best people, we actually learned more than if we did it the business school way. You have your best people be the pioneers to prove whether it's doable or not, and then have them evaluate and refine the best techniques for getting it done. This method of testing resulted in several benefits for us:

- We had proof that the idea could work (or not work, as the case may be) at least it would under the best circumstances.
- We were able to judge the potential of the new concept for the future: If the best manager got only small gains, the potential of the concept was likely very limited.
- We got feedback on what worked, what didn't, and what should be changed. The best managers could help refine the process so that it could be standardized, documented, and used in training.
- Our smartest people found the best way to apply the concept in the practical world, and we got a sense of what the real costs were.
- If the test worked, we had the buy-in of the store personnel who first tested it. They could evangelize the idea among other stores.
- The best managers achieved results that other managers could then strive to achieve. We had a benchmark against which to set high standards, and we knew those high standards were achievable.

## Mining for Diamonds

♦ Insure success! Set up *best-case* examples for others to replicate.
♦ Fine-tune the initial test.
♦ Set the standard for success.
♦ Roll out the new concept slowly and carefully when it works. You will still be ironing out wrinkles along the way. Keep fine-tuning.

*For truly motivated people success is necessary—not an option.*
—Julius Erving (Dr. J), professional basketball player

*Only a fool tests the depth of the water with both feet.*
—African Proverb

# 17 How to Avoid Overreacting to Problems

*My wife, Shirley, and I arrived at the airport luggage area with our friends, Fred and Lillis Beihl, and watched for our bags to get off the conveyor. When Lillis's smallest bag didn't show up, she got very upset. It was the only one that didn't show up and, of course, it was the most valuable. It contained her jewelry. Her husband assured her it had been stolen because "they took the right one."*

*As she became more and more upset, I walked up to her and said, "Lillis, it ain't cancer." Twenty minutes passed. Two things happened. First, the bag showed up. Second, Lillis came up and said, "thanks—you really helped me."*

Such things need to be held in perspective. Losing keys, glasses, and wallet on an almost daily basis is not something to get terribly upset about, notwithstanding the fact that I often lose them and sometimes get very irritated.

It also means the challenges in business should be welcomed because that is why you are there. A problem solver is what you are! There is a big difference between fatal illnesses and business problems. Keep that difference in mind.

## Mining for Diamonds

♦ "It ain't cancer!"
♦ Keep things in perspective.
♦ Enjoy the challenges your business presents.

*A bend in the road is not the end of the road . . . unless you fail to make the turn.*                                        —Anonymous

# 18 Integrity: A Long-Run Profit Maker

*An MBA candidate told my class that she detested her company after they gave her a special day off. Why, when the company had done something nice for all the employees, was she so angry? When asking how to explain the lack of service on that Monday, she was told merely to explain that the phones were down. The next week I thanked her for sharing that with the class. It appeared she got something very positive, a day off, but what she really got was a very negative message about the integrity of the company. She knew that if they would tell her to lie to customers, they would certainly be capable of lying to her. She quit her job the next week.*

This reminded me of the expression both my folks repeatedly told me: "If they'll steal for you, they'll steal from you!" The MBA candidate knew the company would lie to her if they told her to lie to the customers. Similarly, if you expect others to cheat your customers, you can expect them to cheat your company as well! You just can't have it both ways. I'm convinced that one of the greatest things you can do for your team, your business, and yourself is to operate with absolute integrity.

## Mining for Diamonds

If you operate with integrity:

◆ You will be helped greatly in building long-term success.
◆ You can always look yourself in the mirror.
◆ Your associates will love the company for this attitude.
◆ You will draw the right kind of people to the company as your associates spread the word about their workplace and feel comfortable recommending it to others.

*Who steals my purse, steals trash . . . but he that filches from me my good name, robs me of that which not enriches him, and makes me poor indeed.*
—William Shakespeare (1564–1616), author, playwright, poet

# 19 Having Fun

*The store was doing poorly as far as sales went. We would target executive visits repeatedly. The crew was good, and the store was neat and well located. The team was trying very hard to make sales.*

*Finally, one of our more creative executives visited and figured out the problem. The team was trying too hard, making customers uneasy and communicating their tension. He told them to start having fun, enjoying their customers and making them feel at home. Instead of communicating stress, communicate the atmosphere of fun. Stress is like a virus, and you can quickly spread it to your customers by being impatient, curt, pushy, and downright rude.*

*Think of how our potential customers might have felt. They are already uncertain about making a purchase. They may also be very nervous. When people walk into a jewelry store for the first time, they are often intimidated because they don't know much about diamonds. It's easy to scare them away.*

Who wants more stress from an unpleasant, pushy, or haughty sales person, especially when shopping for something like diamonds, a gift that is supposed to convey happiness and love? I quickly learned that the most important side of business is the human side so it wasn't unusual that when one of our stores wasn't meeting its sales goals, we advised the sales team to quit trying so hard and start having fun with their customers.

Here's an example of having fun with a customer. A man came into our Omaha, Nebraska, store and ordered a ring for his wife's birthday. But he wanted to keep the purchase a secret, and he asked the store manager to help with the surprise. The store was glad to help.

The man took his wife out to eat and afterward told her, with a mischievous smile, "Let's go to Helzberg's to look around." At first, his wife was taken aback, responding, "Helzberg's? You waited until the last minute to buy my present?" But no sooner had they entered the store than a clerk greeted them and asked the wife to try on "a new style" ring that had just come in. It fit perfectly and the wife was thunderstruck. Only then did she find out that her husband had picked out the ring in advance and had it sized for her.

Everyone had fun with that put-up job. And that's the way it should be. Include your customers in the fun, and build a relaxed, light-hearted culture. If you think this sounds like Herb Kelleher and Southwest Airlines' approach, great!

When I'm a customer, I don't want to be treated like a wallet with legs. Fun is contagious. Fun energizes your sales staff and attracts customers into a store. And what a pleasant shock to a sales team: "The boss told us to start having fun." That's an order anyone would want to comply with. How can you tell a fun place to shop? Smiling clerks are busily helping customers, answering their questions, making recommendations, and complimenting their choices. And they do not just talk about things the customer can buy. They get the customer talking about the big fish he caught, her vacation trip, or other unrelated stuff. They are making friends of their customers.

There are all kinds of ways to share fun with your customers. One of the best things we did was to invite shoppers to bring their food into the store with them. Ice cream cones? Hot dogs with mustard? No problem. The standard store signs in a mall say, "No food or drink." Ours stated, "Your food and drink are welcome here." We were trying to say, "We are here on your terms. We are different." When couples bought wedding rings, some stores commemorated that day with a photo of the couple for the store album. After all, they weren't buying toasters. They were acquiring memories they would cherish.

Do you have to be creative to have fun? It helps, but it's not necessary. Most of the time you just need to be friendly. Compliment a customer's tie or dress. Perform small favors. We cleaned customers' rings free while they shopped. We put new watch batteries in at no charge. Make your customers feel welcome and at home. It may sound corny, but one of my greatest compliments was when a landlord introduced me as "President of the biggest chain of mom and pop jewelry stores in America."

---

### Mining for Diamonds

♦ If everything else seems to be working perfectly but sales are still suffering, maybe your team is trying too hard.
♦ Create fun! Fun is contagious and it can boost productivity. It creates enjoyable experiences for you and your customers.
♦ The culture and atmosphere of your business may ultimately be even more important than your product.
♦ Study the Southwest Airlines approach to creating fun.

---

*Business is people.*                                    —B. C. Helzberg, Sr.

# 20 What Are Profits For?

*When question time comes up at meetings where I've been a speaker, at times I'm asked, "What are the best things entrepreneurs can do for their community?" In truth, I think the highest priority is for you to make your company highly successful. That includes profitability. Why?*

- *First, to ensure the continuity of the business and the jobs of your associates.*
- *Second, to ensure that the company can go through tough times as well as good times. It's important to have very good earnings in the good times because you know the tough times will come when earnings decrease or disappear. The company will be more likely to survive if you've built a strong foundation.*
- *Third, if your company is profitable and you are able, hopefully you are also willing and eager to share the good things profits can bring with your associates. This includes better benefits and more pay.*
- *Fourth, it will provide great joy for you when you are in a position to give back to your community with your time and financial ability.*

*Although money is not the only motivator (and sometimes a highly overrated one), it's a wonderful way to keep score and it's very thrilling for an entrepreneur to share the company's good fortune with associates.*

Giving is joyful and I always have looked at it as selfish rather than generous on my part because I enjoy it so much! One of my greatest mentors taught me that sharing is a great part of the fun in as much as you can only wear one suit at a time and eat three meals a day without getting overly calorified!

At Helzberg Diamonds we had a tradition of increasing individual earnings as much as 17 percent in the form of 10 percent profit sharing, 5 percent in a check called "progress sharing," and 2 percent immediately vested funds with their match in IRAs. Lots of dollars went into other rewards such as awards, recognition, and celebration, as well!

Devise your own system, but be very careful. Remember that change can be considered a take-away and take-aways are *not* fun, so go slowly. Try *temporary* systems, and don't paint yourself into a corner (Remember, a privilege *quickly* becomes a right).

---

### Mining for Diamonds

♦ Profits are important.
♦ Sharing them is important.
♦ Share in the right spirit.

---

*For this is the journey that men make: to find themselves. If they fail this, it doesn't matter much what else they find.*
— James A. Michener (1907–1997), novelist,
1948 Pulitizer Prize winner, travel book writer

*He hath riches sufficient, who hath enough to be charitable.*
— Sir Thomas Browne (1605–1682),
physician, pilosopher. and author

*Pay peanuts and you get monkeys.*                          —Anonymous

*Profit is a must. There can be no security for any employee in any business that doesn't make money. There can be no growth for that business. There can be no opportunity for the individual to achieve his personal ambitions unless his company makes money.* —Duncan C. Menzies

*Capital is to the progress of society what gas is to a car.*
—James Truslow Adams (1878–1949), author, historian, 1921 Pulitizer Prize winner

# Helzberg Hint **21** A Sense of Urgency

*On Thursday our principal and the board of the char-*
*ter public school we founded (my wife and myself,*
*along with Thomas Bloch, former CEO and president*
*of H&R Block, and Lynne Brown, a community activist*
*and educator) met with our consultant. Two of the ideas*
*that came up were (1) a mirror at the front door so the*
*students could see how they looked as they walked in*
*each day of school as the principal reminded them of*
*the dress code and (2) a sign telling of the $50 cash re-*
*ward each student having 98 percent attendance would*
*receive. We unanimously liked these ideas, and on Friday*
*the school opened with both in place. The students were*
*surprised to see themselves in the mirror when they*
*walked through the doors and were thrilled to see what*
*they could earn just for having good attendance.*

*When my son and daughter-to-be announced their*
*engagement, the first gift came almost the next day. My*
*wife then reminded me that Aunt Myrtle had sent our*
*first gift nearly 35 years earlier. I was amazed. You don't*
*always realize the things you will later remember, but*
*those that stand out are usually the ones that happen*
*first.*

By acting with a sense of urgency, you are modeling the
behavior you want from your associates. You have every
right to expect them to act with urgency and get the job done if
you do so when appropriate.

Have you ever sent a gift and then received a thank-you note right away? Think about the gifts you've sent and waited for an inordinately long time for the reaction, wondering if the gift arrived. The notes took the same amount of time to write. The difference in effect is worlds apart, only because of the difference in the sense of urgency. That is why I urge you to mail a thank-you note to anyone who helps you the day of the help. Warm fuzzies turn very cold very quickly. Shelf life is extremely short.

Nearly any action or communication means far more when done urgently. There is absolutely no substitute for the value of urgent action in the right spot.

---

### Mining for Diamonds

♦ Give top priorities a sense of urgency.
♦ The longer you wait to communicate, the less sincere it appears.
♦ The longer you wait on action that is high-priority, the less favorable the outcome will appear.
♦ If you are unable to give an answer or result as soon as you promised, tell that to the person so they know you have not forgotten, explaining the reason for the delay.

---

*Whatever you must do, or dream you can do, begin it. Do it now. Action has genius, power, and magic in it.*
> —Johann Wolfang von Goethe (1749–1832), poet, lawyer, playwright

*Trust only movement.*
> —Alfred Adler (1870–1937), psychologist and author

# 22 Execution Is the Key, Not the Idea

*Many years ago I attended an outstanding retail semi-*
*nar. One of the speakers was Bernard Edison, who was*
*president of Edison Brothers Shoes, a highly successful*
*company at that time, who said, "Our strategy is pretty*
*good, and our execution is excellent."*

"Whose idea was that?" How many times have you heard that question? I've always been able to come up with many ideas, some of which were totally impractical and unrealistic, though they sounded exciting.

My revelation is that the execution is far more important than the idea. The people I most admire are those who know how to execute. The quality of execution is far more important than the quality of the idea. I was taught at a very young age to let individuals do things their own way as much as possible even if I thought my idea was somewhat better. That advice spoke to execution. People believe in their own ideas and will generally execute those ideas far better then someone else's!

Executing an average idea well will far exceed results of a great idea executed poorly! If the person who executes believes in the idea, the likelihood of success is far greater than in cases where that person is not convinced or excited or committed.

## Mining for Diamonds

♦ Get great executors on your team.
♦ Let them do it their way as much as possible.
♦ Get the heck out of the way, and let 'em go!

*Quality is never an accident; it is always the result of high intention, sincere effort, intelligent directon and skillful execution; it represents the wise choice of many alternatives.*

—Anonymous

*One person with a belief is equal to a force of ninety-nine who have only interests.*

—John Stuart Mill (1806–1873),
philosopher and economist

# Part II

# Decision Making

# 23 Learning and Growing from Your Mistakes

*One of my most prized mentors shared his wisdom: "You don't need shopping centers—you need business districts." I just took that as gospel and did not think things out on my own. The country was about to explode in the malling of America. There was very little agony in our poor decision, very little ecstasy in the result. We elected to pull out of our lease in one of the first 11 covered malls in the United States, a nearly fatal error stalling our progress and causing us to waste years of precious time and resources by pursuing the licensed jewelry department business in discount department stores. Years later we and our advisor realized that avoiding malls was not the right posture. We pursued mall locations slowly at first and vigorously later.*

The lesson learned after taking the advice not to go into the covered malls was that he who takes bad advice is the one and only culprit in the scenario. Advice is advice, not a command. The mall locations later became the success of the company. We had nearly put ourselves out of business by staying out of them.

*One other prime learning experience (read* disaster*) for me personally was in the Helzberg Diamonds mail-order division. I fell in love with the concept that through the use of testing and statistics the mail-order* *business could be built on absolute numerical prediction of volume of business. In those days we believed we were operating at a highly sophisticated level by measuring "recency, frequency, and amount of purchases by individual customer." (What a fascinating contrast to today's far more sophisticated concepts of database marketing.) The more recently the customer had purchased, the more frequent the purchases; the higher dollar amount of the purchase, the more customer value. These were valid criteria, though prehistoric by today's standards.*

*I proceeded to compute how long it would take the business to get from around $2 million to $100 million carrying computations on a small piece of paper in my wallet (I was figuring that would take at least three weeks, I am sure). At that point I never considered that you should not grow a business faster than you can handle the growth. I just imagined mammoth sales increases.*

*Because of my rush to build the business (totally forgetting Dad's "make haste slowly" maxim), I exploded the business in every sense of the word. The level of testing was far out of proportion to the size of the business. It could have easily been limited to a far less significant portion of the business yet still been tested.*

In the mail-order experience I learned that you do not build a business from $2 million to $100 million in a three-week period . . . dot.com users learned somewhat similar lessons more recently. Put a dollar figure on your mistakes. Whatever the learning, you can see it was an expensive education. Figure the potential cost of management mistakes if you are about to take a bold step and see if the risk/reward ratio is comfortable and valid before you make the potential mistake (or home run). Be sure to consider worst-case scenarios.

Most entrepreneurs could dwell at length on their mistakes. The reason to look in the rearview mirror is to divine exactly what you learned and how you will prevent a repeat of those particular errors. Self-flagellation is a waste of time and brain power. Unreasonable buildup of fear, causing you to turn to stone and not innovate, is even worse.

Of course, these are not all of my mistakes—that will take another, far larger book. The positive spin to put on your errors is to see them as learning experiences rather than unproductive errors, just as Thomas Alva Edison did. Just try to keep your batting average over 500.

---

### Mining for Diamonds

♦ When you make a mistake, ask yourself, "What did I learn?"
♦ Ask yourself, "What am I going to do to prevent this from recurring?"
♦ "Make haste slowly."
♦ Misfocus will drain resources and profits from the core business. Will potential gain be worth the risk?
♦ Be sure to consider worst-case scenarios and your ability to handle them financially and emotionally.

---

*The only place where fools may learn is the school of experience.*
—Benjamin Franklin (1706–1790),
statesman, writer, and scientist

# 24 The Paralysis of Analysis versus Knee-Jerk Decisions

*We once had a highly capable retail buyer who needed to replenish our stock of a particularly popular ring. He began a dogged quest to locate the absolute lowest price for this ring. He figured there was a deal somewhere, and he had to find it.*

*Meanwhile, we were running through our inventory of the rings and we were starting to lose sales. Unsatisfied customers went elsewhere. The buyer's fixation with finding the lowest price in the world was not only meaningless, but detrimental.*

*He couldn't satisfy himself on cost of the item, and we grew increasingly frustrated at his inaction. We were to the point that it was better to cut any deal to buy more rings, even if it meant lower profits, to restock our shelves and satisfy our customers. Far better to lose margin than customers.*

*The merchandise buyer had lost sight of the fact that our goal was to sell merchandise. Did overanalyzing prices get him closer to that goal? No. In fact, it had the opposite effect.*

Imagine a person who is so fixated on breathing pure air that he won't breathe what's available until he finds the better stuff. Of course, that person won't be around long.

Analysis is an essential tool for entrepreneurs, but spending too much time analyzing a problem can mire you in the muck of nonessential details. Remain stuck too long and you can become hopelessly paralyzed. How do you know if you're beginning to overanalyze? You'll know it. Nothing is happening. You are not moving forward.

I'm not advocating that you shoot from the hip. In fact, quick draws and snap decisions can be just as counterproductive and can result in quick failures and self-inflicted wounds. Impatience can lead to making half-baked decisions before you have all the facts. Step back for a moment to consider the broader context of the problem, and then choose the best solution available to you at the time and execute the steps you believe will lead to that potential solution. That may not sound profound. It's not.

It's just good judgment that a lot of people forget. They miss the larger picture, the important stuff, as they obsess over meaningless details, as in the much repeated story of the crew members who busied themselves arranging the deck chairs while the Titanic sank. Some don't act because they are afraid of failing. Others haven't a clue about the broader picture. So they focus inflexibly on what they know, even if it's meaningless detail.

The best advice I've ever received about how to resist the paralysis of analysis as well as shooting from the hip is to set yourself a reasonable time limit to make decisions. A reasonable period might be 48 hours. Take out your yellow legal pad. List the issue to be decided at the top. Then, for each potential resolution, list the pluses and the minuses. This is a powerful tool for making decisions. It will force your brain to walk through a reasoning process to reach a logical outcome. It documents your decision process so you can later remember why you came to this conclusion, right or wrong.

## Mining for Diamonds

◆ Fixating on meaningless details can lead to the paralysis of analysis.
◆ Shooting from the hip can lead to disaster.
◆ Set a reasonable time limit to make a decision.
◆ List the pluses and minuses of each potential decision.
◆ Talk to those you respect, share with them what you have thought out, and get their reactions.
◆ Make a decision (remember, doing nothing is also a decision).

*The feeling of having done a job well is rewarding; the feeling of having done it perfectly is fatal.*
        —Donley Feddersen (1915–1979), radio station manager

*They lose that do buy it with (too) much care.*
        —William Shakespeare (1564–1616), author, playwright, poet, "Gratiano, in *The Merchant of Venice*"

*The artist who aims at perfection in everything achieves it in nothing.*                —Eugene Delacroix (1798–1863), painter

**25** Embracing Growing Markets

*After signing a lease in Duluth, Minnesota, I lost a great deal of sleep knowing the market had shrunk by 3.3 percent in the previous 10-year period and worrying that it was still a shrinking market. The major companies in our industry had refused to lease a store there. How could some pipsqueak company know better? Upon analyzing the market, we found a downtown jeweler doing very well. We knew large volume was possible in the market. So we opened in the only major shopping center in Duluth and did well. When a developer tried to create an additional center nearby, it couldn't be done due to the lack of market vitality and growth. Sears ended up adding their new store to the existing center. The Duluth center only got stronger because of the lack of competition.*

The knee-jerk reaction is usually that you should enter growing markets whether they are growing markets for products or growing geographical markets. Analyzing the whole picture told us that the only center in town would be a tremendous draw and we would be in the key location within the center. The danger of proliferation of centers seemed remote.

*In Houston, Texas, when economics were extremely good and the "all bidness" (oil business) was very hot, they seemingly were putting centers up every few*

> *blocks. The town got cut up into little pieces, that is,*
> *overbuilt retail-wise. When the oil boom crashed, every-*
> *one paid including Helzberg Diamonds. Lemming-like*
> *we had entered that hot market and paid the price.*

Sometimes the growing markets where most tend to go create overbuilding and lots of competition. Maybe less exciting geographical or product areas provide greater opportunities! Remember Sam Walton? His initial focus was on small-town America—not the exciting growing markets.

---

### Mining for Diamonds

♦ Do not assume the conventional wisdom is right for you.
♦ "Less exciting" geographical or product areas may represent great opportunities!

---

*Wisdom comes not from experience but from meditating on*
*experience and assimilating it.*
> —Joy Elmer Morgan, editor and co-founder
> National Committee on Education by Radio

# 26

# Borrowing Wisdom and Knowledge about Your Business

*Danny O'Neill left a great job in corporate America because he wasn't happy. He wanted to be his own boss. Inspired by a high school year that he spent in Costa Rica, during which he picked coffee beans, Danny dreamed of roasting and selling coffee. But, as he confessed, the only thing he knew about coffee was that he liked drinking it.*

*Hardly shy, Danny, who has the lanky build of a basketball player and a big ingratiating smile, absorbed everything there was to know about coffee beans and making coffee. He traveled the United States asking questions of everyone he could in the coffee industry. He returned to Costa Rica several times to learn what the coffee growers and coffee brokers do, and to ask farmers what contributed to growing the best coffee beans. He became passionate about coffee.*

*Convinced the best coffee was made by "air roasting" the beans, he bought an air-roasting machine and installed it in his basement. He sat down with business people in Kansas City to ask about best marketing, sales, and hiring practices. He personally visited fine restaurants and stores to build business relationships.*

*He was relentless in his search for knowledge. It didn't matter that there were already giant coffee producers—Folger's had a big plant in Kansas City. Danny wasn't selling a new product. He was selling a product he believed was better. Many people agreed with him. Today, his business, The Roasterie, has its own plant in Kansas City, its coffee is featured in stores and gourmet restaurants nationally, and he has even begun to expand into overseas markets.*

The courage to ask questions is an attribute. Don't be afraid to ask people more experienced than you for their help. They'll be complimented. Many are just waiting to be asked to share their knowledge, especially with young go-getters like Danny O'Neill. You may end up with wonderful new relationships. Want to make friends? Just ask people about their businesses, and let them talk.

We see it daily in the Helzberg Entrepreneurial Mentoring Program, where business veterans gladly help newer entrepreneurs. If you hit a chord with someone you called and you respect their abilities, travel across the country or across the world to talk eyeball-to-eyeball. It just might change your life and your level of success. The more people you talk to, the greater the brew of ideas you will have to marinate your brain.

What an enlightened age we live in. Today, we can access a mind-boggling array of information just by picking up a telephone or clicking on a mouse. Not only is more information available, it's better and often more reliable. Humans have accumulated incredible amounts of knowledge over hundreds of years, and it's constantly being refined through experience and research. Even new inventions build on creative ideas that someone thought about before.

This reservoir of knowledge and human experience creates tremendous opportunities and advantages for you as an entrepreneur. You are heir to the discoveries of many entrepreneurs who skinned their shins trying something new. It is likely other entrepreneurs before you have experienced the same challenges and problems, and found ways to surmount them.

Even so, a lot of entrepreneurs think they have to be pioneers. I define pioneers as people with arrows in their backs. You do not need to invent a new industry to start a new business. Study an existing industry and just do it lots better. Henry Ford did not invent the auto nor did Kinko's invent copying.

You have the experiences of thousands of experts and mentors at your fingertips, whether you're contacting someone over the internet or in your own business community. In most cases, to get answers, all you have to do is ask. What harm is there in asking someone with more business experience if they will help you?

Okay, maybe some will be unwilling to talk with you. But worst-case scenario? You wasted a phone call. What a fabulous risk-reward ratio. Many business people will reach out to share what they've learned.

Now, some people think that if you ask for advice, you have to follow it explicitly. I'm obviously not a fan of that. Some people have a lot of wisdom, but they don't know what's best for you. Why not listen to many people, ponder what they have to say, and then follow your own instincts?

You have to have confidence in this process. You have to believe that at some point you will reach the correct answer. It may not come overnight, though it might. So just relax, and take it one step at a time.

The incredible, wonderful, and unavoidable truth is that seeking the help of others can put you light years ahead of other people who beat their heads against the wall trying to reinvent the wheel. Plus, the relationships you build are priceless. I remain close to many who have helped me. Just remember, one day someone will ask you for your help. Feel complimented, and pass it on.

### Mining for Diamonds

♦ Don't think you have to reinvent the wheel. You don't have to start a new industry.
♦ Allow your brain to marinate all the ideas that come your way, and then do what's right for you.
♦ Learn on the other guy's nickel.

*We are all wholesale borrowers. In every matter that relates to invention, to use, or beauty or form, we are borrowers.*
—Wendell Phillips (1811–1884),
lecturer, *The Lost Arts* 1838

**27** **Gathering Information**

*It was time for another jewelry convention and we had our traditional meeting with the members of "The Twenty-Three Jewel Club," which consisted of two other jewelry firms who were not competitors of ours, Meyer Jewelers from Detroit and Rudolph Jewelers from New York State. The owners were lifelong friends of Dad's and entrepreneurs who had built good businesses. We shared ideas in many areas of the business and always continued building the relationships. These meetings were attended by the executives of each firm and always proved to be fruitful.*

What's really going on in your industry? How can you get perceptions and realities seen through the eyes of others outside of your sphere of influence? It can be highly beneficial to aggressively pursue the enjoyment, as well as the benefits, of building relationships within your industry. It's wonderful to have friends to call around the country to discuss what they perceive is happening in the industry and what is actually happening in their businesses. You'll discover comparable events and noncomparable events; you'll also find where you are missing the boat at times. These peers will be priceless friends as well as reservoirs of unlimited information about your industry. Invite them to come and be critical of your operation; this has been helpful to me and other friends who have used this technique in their industries.

*Another example: Helzberg was in a horrible pickle. Imagine being in the diamond business and not being able to get insurance. We struggled with our insurance carrier for six months. Our insurance company said they wouldn't renew our policy unless we put new safes in every store. The cost to tear out walls and put in new safes was prohibitive. Still, we faced losing insurance coverage for nearly 80 jewelry stores. Finally, our controller called his counterpart at our chief competitor, Zale's Jewelers. Zale's officials wisely knew everyone in the industry benefited from good insurance practices. They put us in contact with their insurance broker and in two weeks we had insurance. Not only were we well insured, we had a better broker, all because our controller wasn't afraid to ask for help.*

Trading information with noncompetitors and sometimes competitors can be very valuable. Recognize clearly that it carries dangers with it as there can be leaks, but the potential advantages can be major. You need to decide what you are comfortable sharing and if you believe the advantages outweigh the possibility of information going to your competitor. If it works, *this technique may lead to some constructive criticism and some big home runs in terms of profit-making ideas.*

I'll never forget when we learned from Rudolph Jewelers at one of our get-togethers, what a wonderful seller the "Mother's Ring" was. The "Mother's Ring©" was a brand new item at that time that we had not heard about. It was actually two wedding bands joined by the birthstones of the children. The ring proved to have an irresistible appeal durng the Mother's Day season. That one idea was a major win for Helzberg Diamonds. Hopefully, we gave Rudolph Jewelers some big winners in return.

Comparing ideas, challenges, and problems is priceless. Fred Ball, a highly successful grocer, set up a small group with five peers who walk through each other's businesses from time to time and tell it like it is to the owner who they are visiting. Everyone understands the goal is not to flatter, but to help. The benefits of this technique cannot be overstated.

This is not a lone ranger program—if you want things to happen you must give your associates ownership of the program—making them part of it as well as yourself. You must make the process work. Let your associates meet with the group. If you want to destroy the execution of the ideas you should do all the talking and give eye contact only to the top persons in the other groups. On the other hand, by letting your associates do the talking and letting peers ask about their own part of the business you have a chance of making it work. The challenge is to defeat the NIH (not invented here) syndrome and make people receptive. You need to design the gathering with your peers and your associates carefully. The temptation will be to cover too many areas. Each person in the process should come up with agenda items well in advance and one person should consolidate and prioritize with their input so the meeting does not try to cover too many topics and adequate time is allotted for the chosen subjects. Lots of this structural stuff depends on management styles within your group.

After each of these gatherings your own team should meet to flesh out which ideas are to be pursued and on what timetable. Then, of course, you need to follow up to check on the progress of each action item with each responsible individual.

Other ways to monitor your industry include subscribing to services that will give you advertising and other materials of competitors and assigning the checking of the Internet in your industry to a responsible individual within your organization on a specific, regular basis. Check out trade associations and see what materials and information they make available to members. Attend industry seminars, subscribe to trade publications. Great places to meet people, even when the seminar is forgettable. The acronym MBWA (management by walking around) is an apt description of another important method you should be using to monitor your industry. *Don't* scorn competitors and *do* have open eyes, open ears, and an open mind.

Visualize yourself as a giant sponge—taking in information from all the sources and balancing it, assessing it, analyzing it, and deciding what actions should be taken. Many enterprises have tragically gone out of business because the entrepreneur had that unfortunate high level of success that creates severe deafness and blindness due to terminal arrogance. These outside resources can help your organization stay dynamic.

---

### Mining for Diamonds

♦ Avoid becoming insulated from the world outside your company.
♦ Go to industry gatherings to network and find a few friends with whom you can comfortably share information.
♦ Set up a peer group to critique each other's businesses. Schedule periodic rotating visits by the group. Set clear ground rules that you want criticism, not compliments. Flattery serves little purpose.
♦ Avoid the feeling that you are a good company and others cannot help you improve. Resolve to go from good to great (see the excellent book *Good to Great* by Jim Collins).
♦ Share these preparations and meetings with your top associates.

---

*A wise person learns by the experience of others.*
*An ordinary person learns by his or her own experience.*
*A fool learns by nobody's experience.*

                                                        —Anonymous

# Following Your Gut: When You Should Trust Your Own Feelings

*Dad used to say that after people pour ice water all over your idea and you still believe in it, then maybe it's right.*

*That was just another away of saying that sometimes you have to follow your gut. I'm talking about that inner collection of feelings and emotions that can, if we heed them, guide us to make good decisions when faced with complex problems.*

*Dad had a restless mind and was always thinking up some new promotion. Often when he was grappling with an idea, he'd walk around with a pencil and a notepad and jot down notions as they came to him. At three o'clock in the morning he would wake up and exclaim, "I've got the answer."*

Like many successful entrepreneurs I've since met, Dad relied on his intuition as much as he relied on his business plans and market forecasts. I don't think he could articulate how it all worked, nor was he one to ponder such things. But he could describe how ideas that welled up from deep within him felt right and true, and was free of doubts and second guessing that might slow him up.

Even now, some of his schemes seem bold and impetuous, but they allowed him to stand out among his peers. In 1920, after taking over the company from my grandfather, he moved the family business into a much larger building and proclaimed himself a diamond merchant, even though he was only 17, knew little about diamonds, and offered nothing more than the usual merchandise.

He understood intuitively that to potential customers diamonds represent the pinnacle of the jeweler's trade. Later on, he bought big newspaper advertisements and staged promotions, including free airplane rides and watch giveaways. People began referring to him as "The Diamond Man," a description he certainly encouraged. (When the Post Office delivered a letter to him that was addressed to "The Diamond Man, Kansas City, Missouri," he used that story to make a great advertisement in the newspaper.)

To some people, his ideas put the company out on a limb. But to him, the ideas felt right, and usually they were right on. Dad listened to other people. He loved mentors. But perhaps, because he started out so young and had to rely on himself, he learned the value of tuning out other people's voices when they became a distraction and listening to that pristine, inner voice that is in all of us.

Your inner voice talks to you through your gut feelings. Nothing mysterious about this. Your gut feelings, or intuition, emanate from your unconscious mind, a repository for all our life experiences and then some. Your mind is a sponge, absorbing everything you feel, taste, see, hear, learn, and experience every hour of the day.

There's no way your conscious mind can keep track of all this data. But scientists have found that your unconscious mind is constantly processing, categorizing, and filing this data away, much as a computer might. So you have all this information available when you need it. In fact, your unconscious mind may have already dealt with a problem your conscious mind might only now be contemplating. That's why we get that "Aha," feeling, when we recognize something that we seem already to have known.

Your unconscious mind has an added advantage. Unlike your conscious mind, your gut isn't fettered by conflicting opinions, self-doubt, or negative emotions that can influence your judgment. When we tune into our inner selves, we are more apt to tap into honest and straightforward emotions and feelings.

It's no coincidence that you hear an executive say, after closing a big negotiation, "It just felt right." When Warren Buffett bought Helzberg Diamonds, he felt so positive about the deal that he cut out the usual due diligence to speed negotiations. Sure, Buffett did his homework, but he also had a strong intuitive response. "I can smell these things," he said. "This one smells good."

It may be hard to pay attention to your feelings and emotions if you've never done it before, especially if you've grown accustomed to letting so-called experts tell you what to do. But try it for a month, and see how it goes. You might look for a quiet place where you can avoid distracting noise. Or do like Dad did and prime your mind with data and then let your unconscious work while you sleep. Some people find it easier to trigger creative ideas by being in a room full of creative people.

Acting on gut feelings can save you time, allowing you to make decisions faster, especially when you don't have the luxury of trying every option. Your intuition can be wrong, but usually not so much that you can't modify an idea or even change course swiftly. Your gut also can provide a check to decisions that don't feel right.

Trusting your gut isn't meant to replace using your conscious brain. The two work together. Your inner voice can validate solutions your more analytical, conscious mind suggests, energizing the decisions, and even making them truly inspired.

## Mining for Diamonds

♦ Ask the "little professor" inside you, "Does it feel right?"
♦ Measure the strength of your conviction.
♦ If you are conflicted, "sleep on it" if possible.
♦ Do not underestimate the value of your "gut feeling."

*My idea of a group decision is to look in the mirror.*
—Warren Buffett, investor

*Great spirits have always faced opposition from mediocre minds.*
—Albert Einstein (1879–1955),
physicist, 1921 Nobel Prize winner

# 29 Priceless Information: Focus Groups

*Focus groups told us that "Jewelry 3", the original name of our freestanding non-mall jewelry stores, was meaningless, the stores were built to look like they were never open, the stores looked like they were still under construction, and the advertising was graded far down compared to the actual store! How did we learn these things? From focus groups of non-customers and customers. Some real shockers for us.*

*Those focus groups gave us a lot to chew on; we had no previous clue that customers were confused by the name "Jewelry 3." We did not think of the branding value of Helzberg Diamonds although I remember more than one of my associates asking why we changed the name of the non-mall stores. I did not listen very well! Since then, changes have been made so all Helzberg stores now carry the same name whether they are inside or outside of malls: Helzberg Diamonds. No more confusion.*

Focus groups are ideal for corralling qualitative information about opinions and attitudes that you can't squeeze out of a survey or a poll. People need more than 30 seconds to explain what motivates or influences them to make choices. For example, you can't learn from a telephone poll the real reason someone chooses to shop at Helzberg Diamonds rather than at jewelry shop X at the other end of the mall, or vice versa.

Most focus groups consist of 8 to 12 participants. They usually share some commonality, which forges a bond among them and makes them more willing to talk. They all might be your customers or all noncustomers, but they are never made aware of who is sponsoring the focus group or the common factor among them. This way, bias is kept out of the mix, because there is neither pressure to be nice if they like the sponsor, nor disposition to be angry if they do not like the sponsor.

Often valuable quality information can be gained from these groups. They can help test new ideas, improve existing projects, create new sales campaigns, and tell you what is important about customer service. Participants can talk freely, using the words that are most meaningful to them to describe what they like and what they don't like. It's little wonder that focus groups have become essential to political candidates as well as to Fortune 500 companies to plot strategies and create images. Questioning is very nondirective, such as, "name the jewelers you have heard of or have shopped at." The moderator lists all the names on a blackboard or on an easel, and each name is discussed separately.

It takes quite a bit of skill to bring out truly individual opinions and feelings in a group setting. Participants will be more likely to tell what they like and dislike than to go deeper and stand out in the crowd for their own opinions. Groups inherently give historical data—what happened, what didn't happen, what could have gone better, etc. However, using projective techniques and other exercises in group dynamics, talented moderators can lead group participants to give credence, or not, to future ideas. This takes some skill, so don't tread this ground lightly.

A good moderator will defuse any building tension and politely redirect the efforts of a member whose dominance is intimidating other participants. The success of a focus group often depends on a creative moderator who demonstrates intelligence, verbal skills, empathy, and patience.

Because a focus group is relatively small, the participants do not necessarily reflect the entire population, but they can provide entrepreneurs with great opportunities to really learn and probe unexpected areas. It's a real challenge in our large and hectic world to keep tabs on what is going on in a market. We can become so insulated that we don't pick up the available clues that can energize our businesses. Your customers and non-customers are often the experts on how you are doing. A focus group can help you tap that expertise. A focus group session can be a cornucopia of ideas for your advertising team. Words can come out spontaneously that give great inspiration to advertising folks.

In addition to focus groups, quantitative research can be done in which people are asked a series of questions and the results are tallied and analyzed. Research surveys have advanced since the days of the knock-on-your-door interviewers, with the Internet being a highly used medium for research.

Professional moderators work best at leading discussions, but if cost is a concern, consider having a college marketing class develop a focus group project.

Research can be helpful. Will you *listen* if you don't like the results? If not, please save your dollars! That does not mean to blindly follow—digest the information, apply it to your situation, and then trust your gut.

---

### Mining for Diamonds

♦ Focus groups are great for gathering opinions and attitudes that are sometimes hard to quantify.

♦ Success of a focus group depends in great part on a talented moderator who keeps the participants on task and prevents domination by one or two individuals.

♦ The advantage of focus groups is in-depth information. The results may suggest further qualitative or quantitative research.

*I think the one lesson I have learned is that there is no substitute for paying attention.*
                              —Diane Sawyer, journalist and anchorwoman

*All wise men share one trait in common: the ability to listen.*
                                                    —Frank Tyger, author

# Treasure the Contrarian: Why Constructive Criticism Is Healthy

*When I put together our first advisory board, one of the first people I called was my friend Bob Schweich, a very wise Wall Street analyst who had been extremely successful. I was straightforward with him and said, "Bob, you are a pain in the butt, so I need you on my advisory board."*

*His advice was always to the point, unvarnished, and valuable. One day he told me why he felt I had been successful. He was characteristically blunt. "It's certainly not charisma, Barnett," he said. "But you listen to what other people say."*

*I could live with that. In fact, I was downright flattered.*

Want to increase your chances of making a great decision? Find someone who disagrees with you. That might sound counterintuitive, but I've learned that getting a contrary opinion from a friend, a customer, or an advisory board member can be a way of guiding you to a more rewarding decision.

Being boss doesn't make you right. Just because you make the ultimate decisions doesn't mean you have all the answers. That sign on your door doesn't make you smarter than everyone else. It just helps people find you.

Sometimes it's hard to open your ears and your mind to other people, especially when you already think you fully understand the situation. Keep reminding yourself that different folks have different perceptions. Theirs might be more accurate than yours. Do this enough times and your ears will tune in automatically to the nuances of what people are telling you.

Fortunately, I've rarely had a problem with people telling me what they believe should be done. My associates would joke that I will go out on the sidewalk and ask 20 people what they think about something. That's true. However, sometimes it's hard to get honest feedback. People you work with may think you only want to hear the good things, not what is really going on. You can become desperate for the truth, so value that person who disagrees with you, for that individual is a true asset. That person may be much more valuable, possibly being the one whose good sense pulls you back from the brink of disaster. Truth is, I've had my share of disasters. Often, they struck when no one was around who was willing to tell me how wrong I was, or maybe I didn't listen very well.

Another thing to remember is that people will soon grow tired of giving you advice when you don't listen attentively or you ignore them. You can't be phony. You can't manipulate people into thinking their advice matters to you, when it doesn't. People know when they're being used. If you don't want advice, don't ask. If you want to gather more brain power around you, listen. I tell my students at Rockhurst University, "Compliments won't help me become a better teacher. Tell me how we can improve this course."

Try these three magic questions with associates, customers, and suppliers, if you really want the truth:

1. What do you like that we are doing?
2. What do you not like that we are doing?
3. What are we not doing that you would like?

## Mining for Diamonds

- ◆ Listen carefully to people who offer you contrary opinions.
- ◆ Encourage honesty and openness in all business and personal relationships.
- ◆ Compliments are nice, but so is advice on how to improve.
- ◆ Use the three magic questions, worded appropriately to your target audience.

*I don't want any yes men around me. I want everyone to tell the truth—even though it costs him his job.*
    —Samuel Goldwyn (1882–1974), American movie producer

*I do not resent criticism, even when, for the sake of emphasis, it parts for the time with reality.*
    —Sir Winston Churchill (1874–1965), British prime minister

# Sticking by Your Overall Objective: Why a Quick Profit Can Be a Bad Detour

## 31

*Bubble watches were plastic watches, priced cheaply at $13.88, that were all the rage at one time. We got in on the fad. It looked at the time like a quick and easy profit, but we came to realize that the customers who came in to buy bubble watches weren't interested in looking at anything else. In other words, we weren't getting any long-term benefit that would help us sell our higher-end jewelry.*

*It became pretty obvious that the bubble watches took more time to order, display, sell, and discuss than they were actually worth to us. In the long run they were a poor investment. After repeated discussions of whether we should continue selling them to take advantage of the fad, we concluded that regardless of the traffic and excitement they created, they did not add to our mission of being the store consumers thought of when they thought of diamonds.*

Who wanted to be thought of as the place to go to buy bubble watches? And what would we sell after that fad faded? Hula Hoops? No way. If it doesn't sell diamonds it doesn't belong.

How many times have you seen or heard a lively discussion over whether or not to take a particular action, cut short with the old saw, "But it makes a profit!" End of conversation?

Shouldn't be. Please add a couple of challenges to that simplistic perception that profit is the be-all and end-all. It's not.

First thing to ask, "Is whatever action we want to take getting us closer to our objective?" Let me say this clearly: The objective of a business is not just to make money. That is the *byproduct* of a job well done. The theme at Ford one year was "Does it sell cars?" At Helzberg Diamonds that inspired, "Does it sell diamonds?"

Second thing to ask, "What is the return on the investment?" Profit, though a simple and quantifiable measure, is far from the whole answer. End of conversation.

---

### Mining for Diamonds

◆ Going for quick profits that divert attention from your objective is a mistake. (Gum ball machines in jewelry stores might make a profit, but will they make you look like the finest diamond merchant?)

◆ Ask yourself if what you are doing now, or considering doing in the future, gets you closer to your long-term objective.

◆ Remind yourself that profit is the byproduct, not the goal.

---

*Obsession doesn't guarantee success. On the other hand, a lack of obsession does guarantee failure.*

—Tom Peters, business writer and speaker

**32** **On Not Giving Up!**

*Winston Churchill said it best: "Never give up! Never! Never! Never!" When Thomas Edison tested and rejected thousands of materials to develop the electric light filament, he showed dogged persistence as much as genius. I wonder if people realize how hard he had to work in spite of the genius label. He labeled these many tests "successful" because he learned that yet another substance would not work as filament. He understood success as a process; failure occurs only when you give up.*

*Each time I leave the runway in an airplane loaded with many passengers and thousands of pounds of luggage and cargo, I think about how unrealistic the Wright brothers were and I actually question the possibility of heavier-than-air flight. Their persistence paid off and I've been extremely gratified that this miracle of flight has occurred each time I've been aboard an airplane that attempted it.*

*Perhaps the world's best example is Tiger Woods. In 1999 he went to his golf coach asking him to change his swing. Acknowledged as the world's best, he went to his mentor/coach and completely rebuilt his swing—to new levels of success. The best keep striving!*

My conclusion: Win, lose or draw, you must keep trying! Yes, even when you succeed you must continue striving!

## Mining for Diamonds

♦ "Never give up! Never, Never, Never!"
♦ Whether you win or lose do not give up. Even if you win, keep practicing, learning, and improving.
♦ Remember, no matter how good it gets, you are just getting started.
♦ Don't be a realist! Pursue your dream!

*Nothing is impossible; there are ways that lead to everything, and if we had sufficient will we should always have sufficient means. It is often merely for an excuse that we say things are impossible.*
—Francois de La Rochefoucauld (1613–1680), French author

*There is always an answer.* —B. C. Helzberg, Sr.

**33** On Giving Up!

*The tribal wisdom of the Dakota Indians, passed on
from one generation to the next, says that when you discover that you are riding a dead horse, the best strategy
is to dismount. In modern business (and education and
government), because past costs are taken into consideration, other strategies are often tried with dead horses,
including the following:*

- *Buying a stronger whip.*
- *Changing riders.*
- *Threatening the horse with termination.*
- *Appointing a committee to study the horse.*
- *Arranging to visit other sites to see how they ride
  dead horses.*
- *Lowering the standards so that dead horses can
  be included.*
- *Reclassifying the dead horse as "living impaired."*
- *Hiring outside contractors to ride the dead horse.*
- *Harnessing several dead horses together to in-
  crease speed.*
- *Providing additional funding and/or training to
  increase the dead horse's performance.*
- *Doing a productivity study to see if lighter riders
  would improve the dead horse's performance.*
- *Declaring that the dead horse carries lower over-
  head and therefore contributes more to the bottom line than some other horses.*

- *Rewriting the expected performance requirements for all horses.*
- *As a final strategy, promoting the dead horse to a supervisory position.*

Nearly every entrepreneur can tell stories of holding on to people too long. Undoubtedly, part of the reason is the absolute dread of firing. Any decent human shares that. Is it fair to individuals to have them in a spot where they will not progress, possibly keeping them from better earnings and a better fit elsewhere? Is it fair to the organization? Is it a choice between individuals losing jobs or everyone losing their jobs when the company fails? If you have been doing your job properly, reviewing and counseling them, the shock should certainly be minimized.

Among our happiest and best decisions were throwing out the dead merchandise horses and finding that the success of the company increased proportionately. We eliminated china, crystal, all flatware, luggage, radios, small appliances, and other non-jewlery items—ad infinitum and ad nauseum. The practice of optometry in a few stores ended. We found the less we sold, the better we sold what was left: fine jewelry. The time to give up on peripheral items had come; we were early in the game of giving them up. The company gained great focus and, doing fewer things, became far more successful.

Certainly one of the most profitable things ever done in our company was the consistent closing of marginal stores that destroyed human resources (who can be motivated in a weak store with the label of *poor store* on it?), used capital, drained central office focus, and really had no reason for being. What a waste of good teammates. A modest turnaround is not nearly as profitable as sending great people to good stores to build them to great so sending the not-as-strong manager to do the impossible makes even less sense. Cut those cancers out as fast as you can. You will not believe how your profits benefit.

### Mining for Diamonds

- Would an alternative investment of time be more profitable; what is the opportunity cost of riding this dead horse?
- Face the music—you are not fooling anybody but yourself.
- The longer you wait to take action, the deeper the hole you have dug.

*Know when to hold 'em—know when to fold 'em.*
> —As sung in *The Gambler* by Kenny Rogers;
> written by Don Schlitz

*That which is not worth doing is not worth doing well.*
> —Warren Buffett, investor

## 34 Judging Your Customer's World, Not Your Own World

> When I was a youth the Firestone Tire Company had a radio program each Sunday afternoon. It was as much a ritual at our house to tune in for the program as it was for thousands of other households.
>
> Years later I learned that when the idea for the radio program was first proposed, Mr. Firestone expressed a lack of interest. "Everybody plays polo on Sunday afternoon," he said. He eventually listened to others and bought the program! I enjoyed the program along with a whole generation for many years.

The point is to listen to your customer, not necessarily yourself, your wife, or your third cousin. We are all *victims* of our own experience as well as the beneficiaries thereof!

Your personal biases can dangerously skew your decisions. (At one point I concluded that if my mother or wife liked some piece of merchandise, it would not be successful!) Judge within the context of your customer's likes and dislikes.

### Mining for Diamonds

◆ Experience can be limiting as well as helpful. Open up your mind! Your customer's experience is probably not the same as yours. Your perception may not be that of your customer.

◆ Research in an informal or formal way the perceptions and habits of your customers. You might be quite surprised.

◆ Adapt the "do not know" attitude of the man from Mars without experience on earth—and listen, listen, listen.

◆ Don't assume what you feel and what you know is true of the world.

*HERE'S A SPECIAL THOUGHT FOR KIDS*
*Did it ever occur to you that a sweater is a garment worn by a child when his mother feels chilly?*
        —Bernard Meltzer, Edward H. Levi Distinguished Professor
        Emeritus of Law, University of Chicago Law School

## 35 Do You View Your Associates As Go-Getters or Slackers?

*Douglas MacGregor gained great renown when he first developed his Theory X and Y and wrote* The Human Side of Enterprise.

*Theory X is the assumption that employees are all lazy oafs trying to get away with working as little as possible, and Theory Y assumes people want to work and be successful.*

The theory is far from outdated and like many pieces of wisdom, it is elegantly simple and has to do with the basic assumption on your part as to who your associate is. I know from my Rockhurst University MBA students year after year that although "obvious," Theory Y is *far from universal* practice in the workplace. Are you a Theory Y manager? Rarely? Some of the time? All of the time?

Theory Y is a principle well worth thinking out with regard to your personal management practices. *Never* underrate the ability of your employees to clearly read your feelings about them.

---

### Mining for Diamonds

♦ Assume the best of your associates!
♦ Trust them. Believe in them. (When you get burned by one person, don't get embittered with all others and lose faith in everyone forever.) Suggested reading: *First, Break all the Rules*, by Marcus Buckingham and Curt Coffman, and *The Human Side of Enterprise*, by Douglas MacGregor.

---

*Success sometimes is more attitude than aptitude.*

—Anonymous

*Leaders know that the "higher up you go—the more gently down you reach."*

—Sheila Murray Bethel, speaker, author, businesswoman

# 36 The Positive Fallout from Enron

*The Enron debacle challenged me to take Dad's advice on finding a positive in this incredibly negative situation. One can only grieve for the thousands who suffered from the cruelty, greed, and dishonesty of the few. After much thought, knowing dishonesty and greed will never cease to exist, perhaps we can be hopeful that employees of all companies will be less naive and hold their employers to a higher standard than ever. Employers may increasingly realize the importance of high standards for purely business reasons if not moral ones. Sins of omission and half-truths are perceived and can destroy credibility earned over many, many years.*

The fullest communication (without endangering a company) with associates of the company, especially bad news, is far healthier coming from you first rather than from exaggerated rumors arriving prior to your dealing with such information. My experience says that associates are most appreciative of information, including negative information, and hearing it promptly and accurately. If you are good to your company associates, your associates will be good to your company.

---

### Mining for Diamonds

♦ Exposure to the corporate fraud and greed of a few companies has highlighted the importance of avoiding misleading
statements or actions by your company.

♦ You must expect cynicism based on recent history and hold
yourself and your associates to high standards.

♦ The more quickly the news, bad or good, gets to your
associates from you, the better chance you have of avoiding
communication challenges.

♦ Omission can be more damaging than commission.

---

*No amount of ability is the slightest avail without honor.*
            —Andrew Carnegie (1835–1919),
                industrialist and philanthropist

*The Enron case is undoubtedly a tragedy but, it is important
not to lose sight of the likely positive consequences of Enron's
demise. As a result of Enron's crash, and the ensuing outrage,
the U.S. Corporate system will emerge stronger and more effective than it was.*                              —The Financial Times

# Helzberg Hint **37** How to Have Uncanny Luck

*An example of luck would be my chance meeting with Warren Buffett on the streets of New York. I was prepared because I had been attending his annual meetings for a few years and felt I knew the kind of person he was. I also was in New York dealing with the very subject I spoke to him about—selling the company and there was top-of-mind awareness of my mission. Add in the unmitigated gall to walk up to him, introduce myself, and offer to sell the company to him and you have an uncanny case of luck.*

There are many interesting and clever definitions of luck, for instance, "where preparedness meets opportunity." Entrepreneurs are expert at putting these two together and creating serendipitous situations that seem miraculous when one looks back at them. Serendipity is far from totally accidental in many cases. You can make it happen if your mind is focused on your goals and you are ready for some pretty unlikely scenarios.

*After a presentation at the University of Kansas, I was asked about luck. I ascribed a good part of my success to it. After I left the class, I thought to myself, "You did that young man a great disservice by agreeing with him about luck." My reasoning is that by ascribing some of my success to luck, though undoubtedly true, I was giving him an excuse to fail, that is, "I wasn't lucky like Barnett."*

Like most successful entrepreneurs, I certainly have had more than my share of good luck. I deliberately lie about this to my MBA classes at Rockhurst University. I tell them I am lying about it! I explain that I am lying in order to leave the responsibility and the onus on each individual for success. My goal with you as the reader is the same.

---

### Mining for Diamonds

♦ Luck is where preparedness meets opportunity.
♦ Be alert for serendipitous opportunities.
♦ Make luck happen by staying alert to potential dream scenarios (they will happen to someone—why not you?).

---

*Good and bad luck is a synonym, in the great majority of instances, for good and bad judgment.*
                                    —John Chatfield (1695–1753),
                                    Revolutionary War soldier

*There is an old saying, 'The harder you try the luckier you get.' I kind of like that definition of luck.*
                                    —Gerald Ford, 38th U.S. President

# 38 Prehistoric Man Looks at Going Public

*In the 1970s we talked about someday going public. In the 1990s when we went to Morgan Stanley to ask what were our ownership options, they said whatever we wanted, that the company was of a quality to do anything including going public. We were indecisive to the point where we simultaneously got ready for a public offering while pursuing the merger and buyout options. We spent a goodly sum on printing up a preliminary prospectus and developing a stock plan for associates.*

Unfortunately, that relates to one of the flaws I find in myself. Sometimes the brain marination takes too long and additional costs are incurred. I live with this by explaining to myself that when you hire someone with any ability you must live with their defects. Although I had little choice when I hired myself on my natal day, this helps me rationalize some of my faults.

At any rate, after wasting the time and the dollars involved in partial preparations to go public, I realized that in my provincial view that move would be the ruination of the company. We would be pushed for quarterly earnings at the expense of the long-run profits and top people in the company would be investing great amounts of time and effort in ways that did not sell more diamonds, such as shareholders' meetings, analysts' meetings, public relations planning, ad nauseum, ad nauseum. Further, I would be publicizing my own stupidity, which is guaranteed to occur from time to time. The price of privacy and all these other factors made not going public a no-brainer for me. I am somewhat stupefied as to why I had to go through such agony and expense to reach what for me became a most obvious decision. Yes, I summarized my conclusion as "that would ruin the company." For me it would have, and since perception is reality, that is valid in my case.

---

### Mining for Diamonds

♦ When considering going public, put pluses and minuses on the yellow legal pad.
♦ Pluses include access to capital markets and possibly the opportunity for financial gain for all associates of the company.
♦ Consider what happens when the stock price falls from time to time, as it inevitably will?
♦ Are you prepared for key managers to spend a great deal of time away from the business (really, in a second business)?
♦ In addition to loss of focus, are you prepared for a whole new category of expense connected with being a public company?

---

*To do two things at once is to do neither.*
—Publilius Syrus (c. First Century B.C.E.), writer

**39** **What Did I Learn?**

*In the 1940s my Dad's brilliant and virtually lifelong attorney, Arthur Mag, went to Washington with the executive vice president of Helzberg Diamonds to visit a federal agency. As they strolled out after the meeting, Mag turned to him and said, "What did you learn?" This is a question to ask yourself after each successful and, especially, unsuccessful experience, "What did I learn?" What is the value in your future whether it be in your family life, your professional life, or both?*

*Helzberg Diamonds opened a very successful store in California and we were, of course, very pleased. We then asked ourselves this question and made a list of the positive factors that we felt had caused the success of this venture.*

If the experience was unsuccessful, the question is, "How can we prevent this from happening again?" If it was successful, the whys are vitally important so you can repeat the performance.

Another trick of learning is to believe that you are going to have to teach the subject in the future. For some reason this technique helps most folks improve learning.

**Mining for Diamonds**

♦ Ask, "What did I learn?"
♦ Ask, "How will I prevent this from happening in the future?"
♦ Ask, "How can I repeat this successful outcome in the future?"
♦ Assume you must teach what you are being taught as a technique to power up your learning.

*The three-word memory course: Attention improves retention.*
                                                                                    —Anonymous

# 40 How to Raise Your Prices

*Many years ago a fascinating economist from Rutgers University named Paul Nadler spoke to a large group of business people. He condemned us for no longer worrying about inflation because it had dropped from 12 percent to 6 percent and told us that you could put a rat in lukewarm water and raise the temperature 1° an hour and he would not jump out even when the water started boiling. When you analyze the compound effect of 6 percent annual inflation, it is extremely serious and would create an incredible effect over time.*

I have never forgotten the lesson he taught us. On the opposite side of Professor Nadler's coin there is an interesting lesson on pricing items that are repeat purchases and on which the price is noticeable and remembered. Turning his principle on its head tells you that when possible and practical, prices should be raised in very minute amounts over a long period, even if the need for an increase does not exist at a given time. Your customers will be far happier with the price if you avoid a major surprise and shock.

Our children's school hadn't raised tuition for many, many years and then was faced with the need for a major increase within a one-year period. The sudden increase created great dissatisfaction within the parent community. Our synagogue did not raise dues when it was not necessary and then was faced with the necessity of major readjustments over a very short period. This sudden increase created great unrest and concern within the congregation. Our school and synagogue should have considered "boiling the rat."

|            | RIGHT WAY<br>(Boiling the Rat) | WRONG WAY<br>(Boiling the Customer) |
|------------|-------------------------------|-------------------------------------|
| Year 1     | $1000<br>6 percent annual increase (41.9 percent increase) | $1,000<br>No increase, then 41.9 percent increase in year 7 |
| Year 2     | $1,060                        | $1,000                              |
| Year 3     | $1,123                        | $1,000                              |
| Year 4     | $1,191                        | $1,000                              |
| Year 5     | $1,262                        | $1,000                              |
| Year 6     | $1,338                        | $1,000                              |
| Year 7     | $1,419                        | $1,419                              |
| TOTAL      | $7,393                        | $6,419                              |

Extra revenue in the example is $974. Result: More revenue and happier customers as well as additional cash flow in second through six years.

### Mining for Diamonds

♦ Small jumps each year! No major shocks!
♦ Do not wait till the price change is necessary; if practical and possible, move in small increments regardless.
♦ Rule of 72: If you divide 72 by the percentage of increase, that tells you how many years it will take to double the initial amount. Example: 72 divided by 6 percent equals 12 years to double initial amount.

*If you own See's Candy, and you look in the mirror and say, "mirror, mirror on the wall, how much do I charge for candy this fall," and it says "more," that's a good business.*

—Warren Buffett, investor

# 41 An Open Letter
to the Entrepreneur to Be

Dear ETB,

I have repeatedly heard MBA students say they could not come up with a new idea and that is what they were waiting for to start their business.

After hearing this repeatedly year after year, I was hit with a blinding flash of the obvious. After sharing my thoughts with these students, I noticed that it resonated with them, thus this letter to you.

Far from needing a new idea, you may be better off taking an existing business and doing it better, much better, than it is currently being executed in the marketplace. After all, Sony did not invent television, nor did Dell invent the computer.

There are two basic reasons: First, you need not be a pioneer and go down a new exploration path. Second, you have the opportunity to analyze an industry, work in it and study it before you embark on your journey. My own perception is that most of the great entrepreneurial successes are based on those who did it better rather than those who did it first.

The point is that if you are truly driven to be an entrepreneur, you need not wait till the skies open up and pour a sparkling new idea on you. You can also talk to customers of those businesses to ask:

- What do you like in the service or merchandise you are getting?
- What do you not like in the service or merchandise you are getting?

- What would you like in service or merchandise that you are not getting?

Your due diligence should also include suppliers, potential customers, and even industry competitors in other areas of the country where you would not be operating. You may also be amazed to find some in your own area that will talk to you. If you can handle rejection, call lots of folks. If you cannot, you better think twice about your entrepreneurial journey—lots of rejection is one of the rewards of entrepreneurship!

I wish you good hunting and much success,

                                                                                  Barnett

## Mining for Diamonds

- You need not invent a new industry or business to be successful.
- Consider doing things far better in an existing type of business.
- Existing businesses enable you to do deep due diligence in that industry.
- The level of risk can be far less when going into an existing industry because of your ability to research.
- The option of buying an existing business does not exist if you want to originate a new one.
- Talk to customers, suppliers, and potential competitors in the industry. Ask, ask, ask, learn, learn, learn—you are now a sponge!
- Keep a diary of all you learned.
- Write down conclusions as you go through this process (it will be interesting to look back and see how they change along the way).
- Learn on the other guy's nickel!
- Pioneers are people with arrows in their backs.

*There are many things that will catch my eye, but there are only a few that catch my heart . . . it is those I consider to pursue.*
—Tim Redmond, writer

*I use not only all the brains I have, but all the brains I can borrow.*
—Woodrow Wilson (1856–1924), 28th U.S. President

# 42 Should You Make the Plunge?

*A telling and insightful movie scene was in "Kramer vs. Kramer" when Howard Duff, as Dustin Hoffman's lawyer, told him one of his favorite ways of analysis was with a legal pad, putting the pluses and minuses on opposite sides of the page. He then showed Hoffman why he had a very poor case in the divorce with his wife.*

The yellow legal pad approach is a good one for many decisions and certainly when deciding if you should become an entrepreneur. There is a price to be paid; you had best recognize it before going in and be sure your spouse and family understand it.

According to one of my MBA students, he learned three things about entrepreneurs:

1. They are control freaks.
2. They are workaholics.
3. They are divorced.

Oliver Wendell Holmes once said, "All generalizations are wrong including this one"; however, some of these apply some of the time and all of them apply some of the time.

In my own case, the workaholic part did apply. The control freak scenario did not apply. In fact, I have condemned myself many times for being an abdicator rather than a delegator. The company executives who reported to me kept me up-to-date.

They basically did what excited and challenged them within the overall direction of the company, which was an extremely simple one, that is, to be the highest dollar sales jeweler in every mall* and to build ourselves as a quality company with the very best personnel on the face of the earth.

However, the "control freak" problem may explain why some entrepreneurs are unable to keep great people who do not want to be controlled and want responsibility and authority!

Potential entrepreneurs must also realize that if they become entrepreneurs, they will be going to work for the worst boss they could possibly have—themselves. There can be no tougher boss, and you need to acknowledge that before putting your toe in the water.

One of the outstanding values of the current generation of entrepreneurs and would-be entrepreneurs is that they definitely give a great deal of thought to the impact upon their family. There is really no getting around it. Being an entrepreneur will steal some family time. You need a highly supportive spouse and your own willingness to lose a certain amount of time with your family. You cannot choose the times for the emergencies to happen, and they will impact your time and life.

The pluses are, depending on your personal needs and values, unlimited in terms of relationships, the joy of enriching the lives of others, the joy of building a quality business regardless of size, and the joy of being your own boss! Your company is best treated like a precious child and treasured in terms of your feelings for your associates. You are dependent on them for your success, and it's safest never to forget this even in moments of anger or whim. You cannot mislead them or your customer, regardless of the circumstances. Few entrepreneurs exist who have not gone through some terrifying times. However you handle them, feel good about it if your actions are well considered and thought through.

---

*After accomplishing the goal of being the jeweler in the mall with the highest dollar *sales per square foot*, we changed our goal to being the highest dollar *volume* jeweler in the mall.

## Mining for Diamonds

♦ Use the yellow legal pad approach to start the decision process regarding your entrepreneurship.
♦ Talk to others you respect, adding pluses and minuses as you go.
♦ Share with your spouse and family your thoughts and get their feelings.
♦ Analyze the financial and emotional components of the situation.
♦ Avoid overly rosy scenarios.
♦ Think out the worst-case scenario, financially and emotionally.

*If opportunity doesn't knock, build a door.*
> —Milton Berle, comedian and television personality

*Small opportunities are often the beginning of great enterprises.*
> —Demosthenes (384–322 B.C.E.), Greek orator

*Most of us never recognize opportunity until it goes to work in our competitor's business.* —P. L. Andarr

*It's never too late to be what you might have been.*
> —George Elliott (1819–1880), writer

# Part III

# Hiring

# 43 Hiring Wisely: How to Choose Good People

*A diamond cutter, in order to judge whether he or she has a superior stone, polishes a little window in the rough so that the kind of quality that exists inside can be seen. Seeing the quality of the rough diamond, he or she determines how best to cut it for the highest economic value.*

Picking out the right individual to hire is a lot like cutting a diamond. You've heard of a "diamond in the rough." A diamond in its uncut state, the rough, resembles a dull, whitish rock. Regardless of how skilled you are at cutting, the rough diamond must be of superior quality right from the start. Otherwise, no matter how good the cutting, you'll end up with an inferior product.

Just as you can't take a bad rough stone and turn it into a great diamond, you can't turn an ill fitted applicant into a great sales manager or marketing director or anything else, no matter how much you wish your training would make it happen.

Think of the interview process as polishing a window in the rough diamond to see what's inside. You can accomplish this by encouraging the applicants to talk about themselves, their skills, their likes and dislikes, their approach to solving problems, why they left their last job, how they deal with changes and stress, and how they interact with people in different situations.

It's easy to tell someone to hire well. It's another thing to apply the right mix of science and art to the undertaking.

Hiring employees, and I mean good employees, may be the hardest task you will ever have to perform. It is arguably the most important. Larry Bossidy, former head of Allied Signal, said, "Good people hire good people." I fear the reverse is also true. The choices you make can either enrich or sap the life of your business for some time. It often comes down to how you prepare for that initial interview. A list of focused questions can direct a job interview in a way that will help you develop an informed impression of a candidate. Merely hoping that chance has delivered just the perfect applicant to your office is not the most skillful tactic.

Hiring the right person requires patience on your part, but if you know who and what you're looking for, the task can be made easier and the interview itself can be made more rewarding. I learned from my mentors always to look for character, values, and people skills. Hire someone who is not only a good fit for the job but, equally important, a good fit for the company culture.

The trainer has not yet been born who can turn poor or ill-fitting material into a success. Nor the diamond cutter who can turn poor rough into the Hope diamond! While individual ability is a plus, and we all love the free-thinking loner in the movies, someone who can't get along with other people in a team setting will create headaches you don't need. Don't forget to analyze fit as well as ability.

When you're excited about your company, it's hard to remain mum. However, a good rule of thumb is to let the job applicant do 80 percent of the talking. Good reporters know that people reveal more about themselves when they are asked open-ended questions, which allow them to talk freely and to offer their opinions on a range of topics. For instance, you can learn about a person's people skills by asking him or her to describe in detail the handling of an office conflict or other problem in the past.

Allowing the applicant to offer information also enables him or her to volunteer answers to questions you cannot legally ask. Be sure to review your list of questions to make sure they are in compliance with current law. Use closed-ended questions (those answered by "yes," "no," or a statement of fact) when you want to know something specific, what the applicant's salary expectations are, or when he or she can begin work. You will also want to know the applicant's expectations of you, just as you will make clear your expectations.

Have several people interview the applicant, so you can get other people's opinions. Other people will see what you might have missed. Interview the applicant on multiple days. Interviewees have good days and bad days, as do interviewers. If possible, have the applicant visit the workplace for a day, so each of you can get a better feel for each other, the job, and the culture. Don't be hurried, and don't succumb to pressure. If an applicant is in a rush and says another job offer is on the table, it's better to tell him or her to take it than to rush to a decision without sufficient information. No surprises is the most important rule of this game, for both you and the job applicant.

Always check references. Another rule of thumb is that a top job deserves 10 reference checks. A simple way to do this is to take the names of the references the applicant gave you and ask them for other references, especially those of peers, customers, and other professionals who know the applicant and his or her reputation. One method that works well sometimes is letting the reference talk about strengths at length, then saying, "Well we all have our weaknesses. What are his?" You need the applicant's signed permission to make a check of credit and police records. There are outside services which make a profession of doing such checks. If the job is a really important one, it can be well worth your time to meet eyeball-to-eyeball with some of your applicant's references, even if it necessitates travel.

In the end, you are trying to piece together a realistic picture of a candidate's past job performances and potential. Interviewing is an art rather than a science. Through friendly conversation you may lead the candidate to reveal basic personality traits, interests, and skills. Since we hire people to perform the tasks they like to do and do well, focus your questions to get the interviewee to showcase the strengths, passions, and successes that form his or her self-image. One strong suggestion. Do not ask about hypothetical situations. Ask only about actual situations, for example: What was the toughest problem you have had (in personnel, selling, with your boss, etc.) and how did you handle it?

Preparing a list of questions beforehand allows you to think through what you want to learn about the candidate. Here are some examples of interview questions, many of which were generously shared with me by other entrepreneurs over the years. They can serve as conversation starters and perhaps give you leads to the insights you need. (Check current legality with counsel.)

- Take a few minutes to tell me about yourself: your education, experience in business, and your responsibilities at your other jobs.
- What subjects did you enjoy most in school?
- What did you enjoy most about school? What teachers? Why?
- Why are you leaving your present (last) job?
- What did you do at your last job? What were your responsibilities?
- What did you like most about your last job? What did you like least?
- Which of all the jobs you've had did you like the best? Why?
- If I contacted your previous employers, what would I be told?
- Other than the position for which you are a candidate, what type of position most interests you?
- What would you say are your best qualities?
- What do you think are your major strengths? Weaknesses?
- What is your goal for the next five years?
- Why are you interested in working for us?

- Why do you feel you are a good salesperson (or executive, leader, etc.)?
- Do you think of yourself as competitive? Why?
- On your last sales job, where did you rank with others? Why?
- Do you feel that you are aggressive? Why? Why not?
- One requirement of the job is to work four or five nights per week? Can you handle that?
- How do you feel about being transferred from the area at some time? Would that create concerns for you?
- If you could have made one suggestion to management in your last job, what would it have been?
- Describe the best boss you ever had.
- Describe the worst boss you ever had.
- What have you done that you're most proud of?
- What kinds of things bother you the most?
- People have different motivations for working. Tell me about yours.
- If you had to choose a new career, what would you choose?
- Use three adjectives to describe yourself.
- How would your subordinates describe you?
- When do you think you will have arrived in your career? What is your definition of success?
- Under what kinds of conditions do you feel you learn best?
- Describe an unpleasant, stressful, on-the-job situation and tell me how you dealt with it.
- We have all goofed in the past. Tell me about your biggest goof. What did you learn?
- What needs would you expect to satisfy by accepting this position?
- What else should I know about your qualifications, about you? Is there anything else you want to tell me about yourself?

- What else would you like to know about the job? The company?
- Why do you think I should hire you?
- What are your expectations of the company? Of me?

Remember to ask follow-up questions as well. For example, if the applicant describes a favorite teacher a certain way, ask why he thinks that particular teacher related best to him.

Using some of these questions and their natural follow-ups may even make the task of interviewing fun. There is no way you can overinvest in honing your interviewing skills. The dividends of hiring the right person for the job are well worth all the effort you put into the process.

### Mining for Diamonds

- Look first for character, values, people skills, and cultural fit.
- Ask open-ended questions that allow applicants to reveal more useful information about themselves.
- Don't allow yourself to be pressured to make a quick, uninformed decision.
- Have other people interview the applicant, and check as many references as possible. Ask references for other references.
- No hypothetical questions, please—real-life stuff only.
- Your headhunter, who gets paid only if you hire, should not be the only reference checker. If Larry Bossidy, head of Allied Signal (now merged into Honeywell Corporation), felt it was important for him to personally check references on dozens of people, you can too.
- 80–90% of success depends on hiring people with good potential. You cannot create the Hope Diamond out of poor material.

*The greatest thing you can do for your competition—hiring poorly.*                    —Bill Gates, co-founder of Microsoft

*For employee success, loyalty and integrity are equally as important as ability.*                    —Harry F. Banks, author

*Never hire someone who knows less than you do about what he's (or she's) hired to do.*
                    —Malcolm Forbes (1919–1990), American publisher

# 44 When to Look Outside or Stay Inside to Fill That Job

*After a particularly tough decision to pass over good, longstanding Helzberg associates, we hired an executive from outside for the job of vice president of merchandising. Time proved it was the right move.*

*One veteran associate who had applied for the job later told me he realized we were right to hire an outside person with the broader skill set for that management position. He clearly told me he could not have done for the company what the new vice president had done. Give good people credit for knowing what's right for the long run.*

Which is better, to hire from outside or from inside the company? Unfortunately, there's no one way to answer that question. It all depends on what your needs are at the time. How do you make this critical decision for the good of the company? Very carefully.

Promote from within and you reward top performers who have already helped you build the institution. This reinforces the existing culture and shows other staff that career opportunities exist in the company for talented people to move up to higher positions. However, hard questions must be asked: Is someone in the company currently ready and able to be promoted to the job?

On the other hand, hire from outside and you may see a wave of new ideas and techniques flow into your company. Due to experience you and your associates do not have, you may experience a new set of business relationships and a fresh perspective on the business. This can be very energizing. At Helzberg Diamonds, when new folks brought in wide-ranging experience, the company truly benefited from the new knowledge and experience. The infusion of new thinking helped existing staff also grow and improve. However, if you hire from outside, it means you must pass up employees who have been with the company and may be hurt or even angered by your decision. On the other hand, if talented managers from outside join you and the company expands and does better, your staff may be delighted (especially when they receive a share of the ensuing profits).

You will need to do the right thing for the company even if it is the hard thing because when push comes to shove (and in today's competitive business climate it always does!), if you don't have the right people in the right positions, you have neglected your duty and harmed the company.

You may lose some sleep over your decision. I know I did, and the friendlier you are with the people involved, the more difficult it becomes to make decisions objectively. I would therefore make the case that, for this very reason, you can't be buddies with your staff. It's agonizing to make these decisions for the good of the company. At a seminar I attended the point was made by saying, "You can't play golf with them on Sunday and fire them on Monday."

---

**Mining for Diamonds**

♦ People of merit exist inside and outside of the company. The right combination of promotions from within and hires from outside can help you build the company beyond your dreams.
♦ Don't promote an affable associate just because you like him or her.
♦ Handle promotions and outside hires fairly and objectively using as the only yardstick, "What is best for the company?"

---

*You must look into people, as well as at them.*
—Lord Chesterfield (1694–1773), English politician

# 45 Hiring the Right Lawyer, CPA, or Other Professional

*I was negotiating a very important contract in 1970. In fact, the conversations were going so well that the individual I was negotiating with felt he could tell me that his attorney said I had incompetent counsel.*

*I assumed competence on the part of my attorney because I was dealing with a prestigious law firm. I did not ask how many of that type of contract this person had done, nor did I ask for references whom I could call or better yet go see to be satisfied. I got exactly what I deserved.*

What did I learn? I did the lousy job, not my attorney. If I had to have bypass surgery, I'd insist on the most experienced heart surgeon available, not someone who only does one bypass operation a year. It should be the same when picking any professional, and at some point in your business career you will need the services of good professionals. You need to know as much as possible about who will be handling your needs, how much experience this person has in that particular field, and check references.

Whether you need to draw up a simple contract or buy a building, having a talented, experienced expert who can guide you through the mine fields can save you big bucks and lots of future problems. That's why you need to hire a professional with the same care that you would use to hire a new employee. If you are concerned enough to seek costly expert advice, you should be concerned enough to check out the individual or individuals who will give you that advice.

Big law firms, just like big advertising firms and accounting firms, shuffle a lot of work they consider routine to their junior associates. It gives these junior associates the experience they need to become junior partners. The problem is that they are learning on your dime.

If the work you need done is truly routine, no big deal. If you are negotiating a complicated contract in which you're investing a lot of time, money, and sweat, you'd better have the firepower you need or you'll take a lot of direct hits.

Don't be intimidated by an impressively long list of partners or the palatial office décor. That's just to impress you. Nor should you be impressed with fancy client names unless you talk directly to the individual who worked with your prospective professional. It's up to you to make sure you get top talent. You know you'd check references if you were hiring a new employee. Well, this professional is a new employee.

---

### Mining for Diamonds

♦ Don't be overly impressed by firm names or client names.
♦ Make sure the professional has done this kind of work before.
♦ Personally check the references of the professional who will actually be handling your needs.

---

*If you suspect a man, don't employ him, and if you employ him, don't suspect him.*                                    —Chinese proverb

# 46 Building on Everyone's Strengths

*Helzberg Diamonds really started to progress mightily in the 1970s. I was fortunate in knowing where my greatest weaknesses lie and was able to find the perfect partner. The new executive vice president, Martin Ross, joined the company. He had a giant amount of experience. He had the right background and installed budgeting (somehow we had survived since 1915 without formal budgeting) and what the sophisticated like to call controls.*

I was fortunate in not having Founder's Syndrome in great part because I was not the founder and I had a great role model (Dad) who knew how to delegate and believed in it. So with our good people we just got the hell out of the way. I believe we really focused on outcomes. Being frightened about survival focuses you on output and not input. As has been said, nothing focuses the mind like knowing you are to be executed in the morning. That was my state of mind.

This taught me the importance of knowing myself and using only my strengths, and letting others use their complementary strengths. I have seen some entrepreneurs fall into a common trap of thinking they have to be the best at nearly everything to be done in the business. Possibly this explains why some managers fail to delegate in ways that would be best for the business.

Why would anyone set such a tough set of expectations and practices? One explanation is simply: ego. It doesn't matter the job or task, these leaders think they should be the best at it.

They may even come to believe erroneously that they are the best at everything. This dangerous condition is appropriately called Founder's Syndrome.

As the founder of a business, you have tremendous control over what work gets done. You may even be doing everything by yourself in the beginning; you may be in a position to make all the decisions. But as your business grows, you encounter new challenges that require a higher level of specific skills and increased time constraints along with your changed priorities.

If the business is a success, you will find it necessary to hire people who possess the strengths and talents needed, but you must decide what strengths and talents to look for. In a world with huge amounts of diversity among individuals, with each possessing a unique combination of strengths and weaknesses, how do you identify the people with the strengths best suited for your company?

The answer begins with you, and it deals with your ego. For optimum success, you must get to know your own strengths and weaknesses. That's a tough assessment for many. But you must be fearless in it, and be completely honest with yourself. Only by knowing yourself will you know how to choose the ideal partners.

Of course, if you already have a staff, you must also assess their strengths and weaknesses in the context of the work that needs to be done as you grow or change direction. Then you are in a position to hire individuals whose skills, strengths, and weaknesses complement or surpass you or your teams.

Every once in a while, a candidate will come along who offers a special opportunity. When this chance comes along, pause. Take a deep breath. Do not perceive this person as a threat. Rein in your ego. Rather than be a jack of all trades and master of none, why not view yourself as a master chef who relishes the task of selecting the right ingredients to build a gourmet organization? Remember, your priority is to hire the people with the best combination of skills and talents for your organization at its present stage, and for its future development.

Remember also that you can't hire great people and then micromanage them. Control freak entrepreneurs don't keep top people. Talented leaders will jump ship when they feel second-guessed, manipulated, and discredited. They need to feel a sense of ownership. You have to give them breathing room.

A big reason for the national success of Helzberg Diamonds is that we hired talented and smart people and then got out of their way. Warren Buffett was so impressed with these same leaders that when he bought the company in 1995, he retained them to manage and run the company. It was a great thrill to us that Buffett felt so much confidence in the gourmet organization that we had put together.

When you take your ego out of the picture you may be more able to make judgments about the future of your business dispassionately. You can honestly answer the question. "What is best for the company." You can accept your own personal limits and rejoice that other talented people can take the company even farther than you might have alone. Ironically, egoless management can be your greatest strength.

---

### Mining for Diamonds

- Egoless managers not only recognize their weaknesses but aren't afraid to hire people whose strengths far outshine their own.
- Consider viewing your role as a master chef selecting the best ingredients to make a gourmet organization.
- Hire talented people and get out of their way.
- If you cannot let others paddle the boat without interference in their areas of responsibility by all means do not hire those strong leaders.

---

*Surrounding yourself with dwarfs does not make you a giant.*
—Yiddish Folk Saying

# 47 Selling to and Hiring Friends and Relatives

*Dad trained us not to try to sell to friends or relatives, which saved unlimited time when I followed the rule. When I violated it, I ended up spending an incredible amount of time (my own and possibly that of associates who helped me) while making an incredibly small amount of money.*

*This counterproductive activity was one that I was most happy to avoid. I also have come to believe that doing business with friends or relatives in any regard can ruin relationships, be awkward, and leave you and your friend or relative with regrets. This is a very personal bias, but one I nonetheless feel should be shared.*

*When you violate this rule (and you inevitably will), tiptoe ever so carefully so you preserve your relationship.*

This maxim is based on my training and experience. Certainly, some industries such as insurance might preach the opposite and have built businesses on selling those they know. We felt fortunate that we were able to operate with the opposite approach. Negotiating with those with whom we have personal relationships can be painful, awkward, and confusing and at times leaves permanent tears in the fabric of friendship.

The unstated question, "Are you my cousin or my business associate?" may confuse business issues. The more business and personal life can be separated, the better sums up my feelings. This does not mean you do not serve those who wish you to them. However, you need not proactively seek that business unless it is an integral part of your business.

What about hiring friends and family? If you are doing it to be charitable, do not. Take care of that person personally in any way you choose, but do not destroy the culture and fabric of the business for a sinecure, a person paid totally out of proportion to their duties.

What about a talented friend or family member who wants to join your organization? There is no surefire solution. This person may be a great addition to the company and its future. You need to have a heart-to-heart talk explaining the ground rules and the necessity of their toeing the line closer than others. Be sure to discuss how things will work if things do not work out. That bridge is easier to cross in advance than at the time of firing. Make written notes for each party. Know that regardless of how friendly the divorce may be, it could damage your relationship with this individual and possibly with those related parties in the family such as a spouse, as in firing your sister-in-law or brother-in law. You'd best discuss the worst-case scenario with your spouse at the initial decision-making time before the individual is hired. See if is realistic to take the gamble that may or may not work out.

Family businesses are tricky and there is a pretty sizeable cottage industry trying to help folks through the minefields they almost inevitably create.

## Mining for Diamonds

♦ Be aware of the perils of mixing friendship and business.
  The two can get confused at times and be counterproductive
  to both.
♦ Tread lightly and carefully when mixing the two.
♦ If practical and appropriate, have an associate handle the
  transaction.
♦ Consider hiring only relatives or friends who may be great
  assets to the business. Keep business and charity totally
  separate. If your goal is to help someone, do it outside of
  the business.
♦ Fully discuss the worst-case scenario with your friend or relative. If it is a relative, discuss it with your spouse. The "what
  if it does not work" scenario must be discussed in detail with
  the potential associate and your spouse.
♦ Know that even though you discussed the possibility of things
  not working out and agreed to preserve the relationship as it
  was prior to the hiring, it will inevitably change when you
  pull the trigger. Be prepared and prepare your spouse.
♦ Analyze fully the risk–reward ratio of hiring your friend/relative.

*A friendship founded on business is better than a business
founded on friendship.*

                                        —John D. Rockefeller, businessman

# Part IV

# Inspiring

# 48 Recognizing Great Work: How to Motivate Associates

*At Helzberg Diamonds, we gave careful attention to the people who were at the front lines. The top 25 sales associates each month received a small gift with a handwritten personal note from me. I enjoyed shopping for and sending these gifts, which were mailed to each associate's store for all to see. This way, these winning associates were recognized by their colleagues as well as by the company. Seeing these gifts also motivated other associates to raise their performances to win similar recognition the next month. Although some of the gift items were expendable, even sharable, such as giant cans of popcorn, many were more permanent and personalized mementos, giving an individual an added opportunity to recount the accomplishment to a friend or neighbor when asked about the gift keychain or clock.*

The more effective a relationship you have with your staff, the better you will know what kind of recognition reinforces the behavior you want to encourage. One day I wrote the post office (yes, the post office) about some wonderful service I had received from a particular individual. The next time I saw him he told me how much he appreciated it, that it was food for the soul, and he nearly cried. When you have something nice to say, why not say it?

Backslapping "attaboys" are not meaningful and can actually be insulting to any intelligent person. Specifics are, such as taking great customer comment cards mailed to me and sending them directly to the individual who got the great compliment from the customer with a personal handwritten thank-you note. These were proudly displayed on the bulletin board in each store and seemed to stay up forever. Did they inspire more of the same? You decide. I admit I loved doing it, but I felt it was great positive reinforcement. Yes, when the comments were negative we also followed up.

Great teachers understand the power of positive reinforcement to increase desired behaviors, and so do great entrepreneurs and managers. Unless you were a very savvy child, you didn't realize that the teacher who praised you was using a scientifically proven motivational technique, but you felt its powerful effect.

In business, the sincere use of positive reinforcement has proven effective time after time. Recognizing your staff for good work buoys their attitudes and boosts effectiveness. To be effective, positive reinforcement should be timely and specific to the behavior you are trying to reinforce. Just telling someone, "You're doing a good job," doesn't sufficiently tell someone what he or she is doing well. More importantly, it doesn't effectively communicate that you paid careful attention to the employee's performance. Vague and overly elaborate praise loses its motivational power and begins to be perceived as less than sincere. In contrast, telling a person, "I appreciate the way you responded to that angry customer," recognizes a specific behavior and motivates the person to build on that strength. Timeliness of reinforcement is important as well. If you wait too long to recognize someone, the behavior you wanted to encourage may no longer even be occurring.

Don't underestimate the power of personal thank-you notes. While typed notes are okay, the more personalized the notes, the better. The few seconds it takes to write a personal note or a handwritten P.S. on a typed note tells the recipient you care, that you personally noticed the achievement. I'm amazed at how easy and effective this technique is—and how rarely it's used. However, the books by and about some of the great business leaders retell the story of handwritten notes. Sometimes, they are saved for years.

Is money a motivator? According to management research, the answer is "sometimes." It depends on the employee, the circumstances, the amount, and how one perceives the value of money. Financial bonuses can provide rewards when carefully tied to the right things. Even so, salaries by themselves are not always strong motivators.

Dr. Frederick Herzberg, in his classic 1968 article in the *Harvard Business Review*, addressed this issue. When salaries are fair, he wrote, they are no more motivating than a clean restroom. Thus Herzberg maintained that money is merely "hygiene." But when people perceive salaries to be unfair, then money becomes a "dissatisfier."

Competition can provide a lot of motivation. Being number one is a big part of this brew, and people with winning attitudes get results. I gleefully remember the reaction of one of our managers upon receiving his bonus. He immediately asked, "Is this the biggest?" Now, some bosses might have thought him to be quite rude. I thought him a winner. We asked ourselves, "Would he rather have a #1 slot and get $1000 or the $10,000 he actually got?"

Appreciation sincerely shown is a powerful motivator. Critical words, on the other hand, land sharply and are not easily forgotten. Some managers believe that in order to control their staffs they have to be stingy with praise. Some even think the only way to get their people to perform is to kick butt. These misguided and antiquated techniques might work temporarily, but not for long.

Ask yourself, how long you would be motivated by a supervisor who never recognized you for performing well or, worse, nitpicked to find negative things to tell you? Sadly, this type of misguided boss is far too common. If you are an entrepreneur, it may even have been such a boss that convinced you to become an entrepreneur.

Good teachers know this, good parents know this, good managers know this, and the greatest sales organizations know it too. Read up on Mary Kay Ash and Ewing Kauffman and the organizations and successes they built with recognition. You need not be original—just do it!

## Mining for Diamonds

- Recognition reinforces behavior. Tie verbal, material, and symbolic recognition to the right stuff.
- Recognition should be specific.
- Don't forget the personal touch. A handwritten note can be a powerful motivator.
- Promote competition. Find achievements to reward.

*After a person has food, clothing and shelter, the greatest motivational force of all is appreciation.*

—E. M. Kauffman (1916–1993),
pharmaceutical entrepreneur

# **49** Encouraging High Achievers

*The classic story of Dr. Roger Bannister is the ultimate tale of goal setting. The four-minute mile was generally acknowledged to be an impossibility for the human body. No one ever made a rule that the four-minute mile could not be broken. Yet, it was widely believed that human beings lacked the physical capacity to break that barrier. But Dr. Bannister, being one exceptional athlete, set his sights on that goal and did break it. One year after Roger Bannister ran his miracle mile, 37 other athletes did it, too—even two runners in one race!*

Goals changed and accomplishments changed. All it took was one high achiever to set the standard for success, inspiring thousands of young high school runners to see that it could be done.

*One day our store manager in Greenspoint Mall in Houston, Texas, asked whether my goal of doubling the sales volume on a per store basis within a five-year period was realistic. I told him that I was absolutely not being realistic and that being realistic was not my job. (We did double it although it took longer than five years!)*

Because the world continually changes, whatever one is doing today is not going to be good enough for tomorrow. Toyota calls it "continuous improvement." Sometimes your high achievers will set standards far beyond yours, throwing out old myths in the process. People are the answer to almost all your challenges.

Imagine a sporting event in which neither team knew what counted as a goal? It would be ludicrous. Players would wander around aimlessly. No one could keep score, so there'd be no way to measure the outcome of the game and no feeling of accomplishment for anyone.

It's the same in business. Setting clear standards of performance tells people what the goals are. Standards allow us to measure our performances and they tell us how far we've come and how far we have to go to reach our destination.

They are essential to a successful business. At Helzberg Diamonds we gave a lot of thought to performance standards. We found that when used in a positive way, high performance standards motivated high achievers to push the envelope of their abilities. One early goal was to have $1 million average sales per store. When we hit that, the goal became $1.5 million . . . and of course, after achieving that goal the new goal became $2 million. This was no secret. We communicated it ad nauseum. We quit looking at the competition's average volume per store and competed with our own figures every year.

Are you using the right benchmarks? If your company compares itself only to its industry and quits striving beyond— malaise has struck. If the company has excelled and challenges itself with its own accomplishments and seeks the next level, it can be continually challenged.

These are illustrations of the principle of minimum contentment and maximum success. Regardless of current accomplishments, the great manager's attitude is, "We're just getting started." Your journey never ends. Get your own benchmarks!

Build a unique level of success within your personal career and your company.

Individual sales records were rewarded with trips to the home base, parties at our family home, and the most fun and dramatic celebrations imaginable. Now $1 million in sales has actually been achieved by individual salespeople! We were delighted to reward high achievers, to keep them motivated. They were setting the standards for the entire company.

Most sales competitions are like a pyramid with only a few winners on top. The bulk of the participants know beforehand they are unlikely to win and therefore are turned off. It is important to have lots of winners. IBM had competitions in which participants had a good chance of winning and knew it. Instead of competing against other sales people, each sales person had his or her own goal (because of different territories, histories, length of service, customers, and competition). Meeting or exceeding the individual goal resulted in most of the folks being winners. IBM rewards a major part of its sales force as winners. Obviously, in areas where the numbers do not do the whole job, it will be more complicated to set standards. Some may be judgment-based requiring subjective input.

Good people want to earn rewards. They don't want handouts. They resent it when rewards are distributed randomly, unrelated to achievements. Individuals should be allowed, enabled, and empowered to earn dollars, acclaim, and awards. Standards should be tough, fair, and apply to everyone equally, so the resulting rewards are meaningful.

Please note that the title of this chapter is Encouraging High Achievers. You must work on what is left in people, not what is left out. These techniques will not turn the unmotivated into the motivated. Not everyone is energized by high standards. Some will try to slide through by doing the minimum. You can't change them so focus instead on your high achievers. They're the ones who will make your company a success.

**Mining for Diamonds**

♦ Set high, attainable standards.
♦ Celebrate your winners.
♦ Design a variety of ways that encourage winners to win.
♦ A high percentage of your employees should come in as
  winners, so set up your reward system accordingly.

*Aim high! It is no harder on your gun to shoot the feathers off
an eagle than to shoot the fur off a skunk.*          —Troy Moore

*If you don't believe in miracles you are not a realist.*
                              —David Ben-Gurion (1886–1973),
                              the first Prime Minister of Israel

# 50 Leaving Your Campsite Better Than You Found It!

*When I went to Camp Nebagmon in Wisconsin at the age of 12, I learned from our late beloved camp director, "Muggs" Lorber, "Always leave your campsite better than you found it." We youngsters thought he was talking about the campsites we used when we camped out. So we carefully picked up trash and properly put out the campfire, leaving our campsites in great condition for the next campers. Forty years later I realized he was talking about much more. He was telling us that whatever we touched during our lives should be better when we leave it.*

This rule has a hard time finding places where it does *not* apply. It works well in all you do, and of course, you get the ultimate dividend—the satisfaction of knowing that you left your (you fill in the blank) better than you found it at the beginning.

In a sense, Warren Buffett has helped to set the example for corporate America by proving that corporate behavior can be open to the closest scrutiny and reveal something to be proud of. The Berkshire campsite and the campsites of the companies over which he has some level of control are examples. His conduct has been exemplary, whether you consider his $100,000 salary, his lack of stock options, his urging companies to expense stock options, or his unique plan allowing shareholders to send their pro rata share of corporate contributions to the charities of their choice. The company budgets charitable contributions and lets each shareholder decide what charity his or her share goes to. His conduct should help to light the way to more responsible conduct on the part of other CEOs and raise the expectations of shareholders, as opposed to what has been exposed at the Enrons, Tycos, Arthur Andersens, and other such denizens of our business landscape.

There are unlimited opportunities in your business and your life to leave your campsite better. Your opportunity certainly includes improving employee benefits and treating employees as the assets they are rather than as folks whom you want to pay the least you can. It includes the nonmonetary rewards that evidence themselves in the proper treatment of others.

Leaving a company better than you found it at the beginning helps make the system work better and makes more jobs, more expansion, more companies profitable, and more bonuses for more individuals. That is doing far more than satisfying greed. It helps build America. Further, as you help one generation, the next one starts from a higher point on the ladder, whether it's education or income or just the pure enjoyment of life.

Thank you, Muggs, for a great inspiration that has provided lifelong guidance for me.

---

### Mining for Diamonds

♦ Always leave your campsite better than you found it.
♦ Each year, each month, each day is a new opportunity.
♦ When you help one generation, you are helping future generations and their progeny.

*SUCCESS*
*To laugh often and much;*
*To win the respect of the intelligent people and the affection of
  children;*
*To earn the appreciation of honest critics and endure the betrayal
  of false friends;*
*To find the best in others;*
*To leave the world a bit better;*
*To help in leaving a better social condition;*
*To know that even one life has breathed easier because you have
  lived.*
*This is success.*

—Ralph Waldo Emerson (1803–1882),
author, poet, philosopher

**51 Ownership**

*When my brother Charles was about 23, my Dad gave
him the responsibility of merchandising the Longines
watches. Charles thought he was way too young and
inexperienced to take on such a task and indicated as
much to Dad. Without blinking an eye, Dad told him
that if he didn't do it now, in five years he would still be
young and inexperienced, so he should just take ownership and responsibility for it now doing things as he
(Charles) saw fit and not wait. Charles merchandised
the watches in his own way and did a fine job, clearing the
way to take on new responsibilities without hesitation.*

Although many of Dad's practices I find to be common
among successful people, this one I do not. His concept of
what to do in the situation in which you have an idea and the
person responsible for the idea's execution has a different idea
of how to get something accomplished was quite unusual. He
always said to let them do it their way even if you think your
way may be a little bit better.

This speaks to the concept of ownership of the project by
your associates in applying the solutions and procedures used in
the business. Dad knew that execution is far more important
than the idea, and he insured better execution through belief in
others. Motivation and execution will tend to be far better if the
individual applies his or her own ideas to the challenge. This
concept of ownership is the one that can ignite the spark in
your associates, get the job done better than you can expect,

and reward them with the joy of accomplishment. Is also may be the toughest for many entrepreneurs to embrace.

Pure psychological ownership can fire up enthusiasm and leadership qualities in those around you. It will point you to future leaders. This concept says, "I trust you, I believe in you," and it can motivate the living hell out of people.

Ownership is key to success. Give it a try—it is not a 20-year commitment to try it once or twice!

---

### Mining for Diamonds

♦ Enhance performance by giving ownership.
♦ Let them do it their way.

---

*Work is love made visible.*                    —*The Prophet,* Gibran

*When a man decides to do something he must go all the way, but he must take responsibility for what he does. He must know first why he is doing it and then he must proceed with his actions with no doubts or remorse.*
                              —Carlos Castañeda (1925–1998), author

**52** **On Humility and Arrogance**

*Some people have said to me in the past that I possessed
humility. That always reminds me of Winston Churchill's characterization of Clement Attlee, "He is a humble man and he has a great deal to be humble about."*

It is incredibly important that you make other people the
stars of the show and not yourself. This includes little sub-
tleties like sometimes not inviting them to come to your office,
but rather going to their office. It also includes never answering
the phone if you happen to be in your office with them unless
it is an absolute necessity (your answering the phone means that
you are important and your associate is unimportant and you
can waste their time if you wish) and the usual courtesies of
how you would deal with social friends.

The benefits of absenting your ego are virtually unlimited
and will help to give you the thrill of helping others to develop
in wonderful ways. Perhaps I have been fortunate to lack the
self-confidence to believe that many of the good things that
happened to our company were due to me. I felt I realistically
saw why these things happened and realized that my contri-
bution was selecting great teammates, setting a clear and simple
direction, staying out of their way, and possessing extraordi-
nary luck.

Any honest and accurate appraisal of Helzberg Diamonds'
progress through the years would have made that clear. Our
success was due to our officers, managers, and associates. I was

fortunate to be unable to achieve any level of confidence or arrogance because I realized how little so much of the success of Helzberg Diamonds was due to me personally. My "humility" was merely an honest realization of what had created our success.

The day you start to believe your press will likely start your downhill slide! Ego can be something that can be highly productive for you if you leave your ego on/off switch in the off position. This saves a great deal of time as well as creating far higher productivity in those around you.

Arrogance is counterproductive because arrogant people tend not to listen to and learn from others. Arrogant people are a tremendous turnoff to folks who work with them, cutting off real communication.

Most of us know so little about the world, no matter how deeply we know about one small part of it, that we really don't have the right to be arrogant. Keep this in mind as you gain more and more success and realize that maybe success occurred in spite of the dumb things you've done (as in my case) as well as perhaps because of some wise things others have done and some very good luck!

---

### Mining for Diamonds

◆ Arrogance is counterproductive. Avoid it.
◆ In addition to working with great associates and professionals, I realize that our success came from other sources over which I had no control:
  ◊ Good economic times during most of the period when I was at the helm.
  ◊ Severe mistakes and financial problems of competitors.
  ◊ Population growth at the jewelry-buying age levels.
  ◊ Just plain good luck!

*One who desires the attention of others has not yet found himself.*
—Rav Shlomo Wolbe, Israeli rabbi

*The proud man counts his newspaper clippings—the humble man, his blessings.*
—Bishop Fulton J. Sheen (1895–1979),
author, speaker, writer

**53** **When Bad News
Is Good News**

*In 1965 we received a "Dear John" letter from Kmart
Corporation. It indicated our leases would be discontinued in all of the of Kmarts in which we were operating licensed jewelry departments. Initially, we were
quite upset. That was the day we sat down and realized
our future was in long-term leases in shopping centers
and not with 30-day cancelable leases in discount department stores.*

*Actually, the Kmart people were far more generous
than our contract required and gave us many months to
discontinue the operation. When I asked for relief on
the December rent, they gave it to us although they had
no obligation to do so. I will never cease to be grateful
for their treatment of us at that difficult time.*

*We proceeded to close 24 licensed departments and
closed 14 of the 15 then-existing Helzberg stores, moving them, when possible, to shopping malls in each market. We had the fun of actually reinventing the company
by moving or closing 38 of 39 locations. Thank you
Kmart for that wonderful letter! It was the start of
transforming a struggling company into a success.*

*W*hatever *happens* figure out *why* you were "kicked upstairs"
(another of Dad's sayings) and think of it in a *positive
sense*: then go forward!

This approach turns bad news into good news. I often tell
myself, "Thank God I have diabetes. I cannot weigh 500 pounds
and must keep in shape!"

---

### Mining for Diamonds

♦ Bad news is good news! How? Figure it out! Then go
   forward!

---

*We were kicked upstairs.*                        —B. C. Helzberg, Sr.

*A problem is a chance for you to do your best.*
                          —Duke Ellington (1899–1974),
                            composer, band leader, piano player

# 54 Expectations

> *I called the manager, sharing my pleasure at the sales
> of one particular saleslady. "What happened?" I asked,
> because she had been underperforming for months. His
> reply: "I told her she needs to sell an average of $60 per
> hour at the minimum to earn her keep."*

I admit to being a little thunderstruck because I thought it was standard procedure to let our salespeople know the minimum sales per hour average they were being paid for. But I was happy he had gotten the job done.

I often wonder what percentage of the world's problems would cease to exist if the *expectations* of all parties were discussed. That is why this has become a favorite word of mine—clear expectations can detoxify a potentially dangerous situation before the disaster even begins to happen. Yet, we rarely compare expectations with those we work for and with, or are married to.

Asking expectations of applicants at the first interview and stating those of the company to him or her could save much grief later—sometimes preventing the hiring of the wrong individual and sometimes showing them that the company is not the right place for them.

It might be tremendously advantageous to write out for yourself the expectations in advance of the interview. This will force you to think more completely about them. The fact that change is constant and expectations may change from time to time must be stated at the time of this first conversation so that

you never hear "that was not part of the job when I was hired."
Never "gild the job"—if anything make it sound tougher than
it might be.

Equally important, listen to the expectations of your interviewee. Your will learn a lot more than their expectations about
them if your antenna is operating properly. Working very
hard at listening can be of great value to you in your decision
making. Is their prime interest benefits and money or the job?

Consider writing out the expectations of both parties and
putting them in the employee file when they are hired. That might
be beneficial at some point—including of course that expectations can change.

Make *expectations* a regular part of your vocabulary and
agenda. The effects will be very positive!

---

### Mining for Diamonds

♦ Discuss your expectations of others in detail.
♦ Understand potential employee's expectations.
♦ Avoid surprises by clearly communicating your expectations.

---

*A master can tell you what he expects of you. A teacher, though,
awakens your own expectations.*
                                                    —Patricia Neal, actress

**55** Unintended Consequences

*One of the models of great crisis management is the Johnson & Johnson handling of the Tylenol poisoning case in Chicago. Tylenol on the shelves of a store had been tampered with and poisoned. Deaths and illnesses ensued. J&J pulled Tylenol off the shelves all over the United States.*

*Obviously, their management took unintended consequences into account when, rather than pulling Tylenol off the retail shelves only in Chicago where the tampered Tylenol poisonings had taken place, they pulled Tylenol from shelves all over the country. They realized that the guilty parties or copycats would very possibly replicate the crimes that had taken place in other areas. They salvaged a great brand name by making the right decision at the outset. The product returned to the retail market in tamperproof formats.*

That crime had other unintended consequences in terms of the packaging costs of many product lines. They were changed to tamperproof formats, and the costs in most cases increased.

*We had decided that the future course of Helzberg Diamonds was indeed in diamonds and that we should discontinue non-jewelry lines of merchandise. Over a brief period of time we phased out innumerable lines of merchandise such as china, crystal, silver, luggage, and radios. Since our managers were on profit bonuses, we explained that we believed their dollar volume of business would decrease but their profits would increase.*

We were wrong. Both volume and profit went up. This was when we found out that less is indeed more. The very pleasant unintended consequence of getting rid of other lines of merchandise was that sales actually increased and we were on the way to a far better future.

*I recall the story of the eons-ago firing of a long-term executive who had a reputation of cruelty to other employees. Rather than being happy that he was gone, the translation to the other employees was that nobody's job was safe, a consequence that was most unexpected.*

Most stories of unintended consequences are horror stories. One thing any successful entrepreneur must do is think of the unintended consequences of the actions that he or she plans to take. This must become second nature for you. After attending a seminar at the Menninger Foundation, one of our executives repeatedly quoted the mantra, "When you light up one button some others automatically turn on."

Even the most positive things like a raise can have such consequences as "I thought it would be more" or anger on the part of those who did not get a similar raise. You dare not assume that any action will not have other consequences.

Thinking out the unintended consequences is not necessarily for the purpose of changing your direction (although that will happen sometimes), but rather being prepared for what may come from the action you are about to take or better yet, planting some antivenom if possible before the action is taken. You should not be surprised when the unintended consequences take place. You may be able to blunt the effect by referring to the fact that "there will be no more layoffs" or whatever the facts are. However, you must be accurate or lose all credibility.

---

### Mining for Diamonds

♦ You must automatically think about unintended consequences with each action you take.
♦ When you light up one button, what others could light up?
♦ Sometimes unintended consequences can be dulled or avoided by your vaccinating your constituency against a rumor or other problems.
♦ Proactivity is far better than reactivity, when possible.

---

*What we anticipate seldom occurs; what we least expect generally happens.*

—Benjamin Disraeli (1804–1881),
novelist and British Prime Minister

# Part V

# Communicating

**56** Digging Out the Answer

*Our friend Ted was plagued by stubborn skin infections
some years ago. Nothing seemed to bring relief. So his
frustrated physician took the problem to a roundtable
of physicians who met weekly at Massachusetts General
Hospital to discuss problem cases.*

*One member of the group was a pediatric nephrol-
ogist, a physician who specializes in children's kidney
diseases. When he heard the symptoms described, he
suggested that Ted try a special soap, Hibiclens. With
nothing to lose except his discomfort, Ted started using
the soap whenever he showered or washed his hands.*

*The symptoms began to disappear as mysteriously
as they first appeared. Within a few years Ted was able
to stop using the soap, and he has been free of the skin
infections for more than 15 years.*

*Ted had previously gone to all the appropriate skin
specialists. Yet the answer came from outside the expected sources. Ted would never have thought of going
to a pediatric nephrologist, but his physician had the
courage and wisdom to ask other experts to help him
brainstorm a solution.*

I'm always delighted when someone in a group can view a scenario in a wholly different way and suggest an unexpected
solution to what seemed an intractable problem. I've seen it
happen so often I'm convinced nearly any problem can be

solved by bringing together a variety of smart people to brain-storm. My Dad quoted a slogan for the tactic that was printed on the agenda for every executive meeting, "All of us know more than one of us."

A fresh viewpoint can even change the perception of a prob-lem. Think how often you have waited a long time for an ele-vator. It can seem to take forever to get to your floor. One solution is for the building owner to put in more elevators or speed up the ones already there, but that might be impractical or costly. In an example of what famed journalist Arnaud de Borchgrave calls "vertical thinking," one idea involved a sim-pler and cheaper alternative. If you put mirrors in the waiting area, people will primp while they wait and the perception of time changes. This solution recognizes that perception is reality, and the goal is to change the perception of the waiting time.

To make brainstorming work, you have to respect every-one's ideas. If you never listen, if you never follow anyone else's idea, then it's counterproductive to hold brainstorming ses-sions. (This doesn't make you a bad person—just one who should definitely not use this technique.)

As to the size of the group, there's no magic number. It should be small enough to nurture rapport. You want people to feel comfortable enough to talk, so you want to set a respectful tone that is conducive to sharing ideas and free of sarcasm. Humor is great but not to the point that people start feeling defensive.

Oh, and leave your ego outside. I always want to be the dumbest guy in the room. You're not supposed to be the answer person. You want other people to express their good ideas. That's one reason you hire smarter people than you (and they will never disagree on that)!

## Mining for Diamonds

♦ All of us know more than one of us.
♦ A fresh viewpoint can change your perception of a problem, leading to a more creative solution.
♦ Respect for the opinion of each person in the group encourages greater sharing.

*There is always an answer!*                    —B. C. Helzberg, Sr.

*A new idea is delicate. It can be killed by a sneer or a yawn; it can be stabbed to death by a quip and worried to death by a frown on the right man's brow.*

—Charles Brower,
president, Batten Barton Durstine and Osborn
(advertising agency)

# 57 How to Kill New Ideas and Communication

Meetings come and meetings go, and many prove to be non-productive. Sometimes institutional memories are not used properly. Perhaps at times those possessing the memories feel they would somehow be diminished if some new idea was made to work. How many ideas work the first time out? Fortunately, they were not there when the new idea person tried to walk. They might have said, "You are just going to fall down!" Numbers 1 and 2 below are excellent examples of this phenomena.

You hope your naysayers are constructive, sound people. Normally, there are some folks who employ phrases to kill a new idea. You could lose some value when a good idea gets lost because of negativity.

Will reminding folks of these seven devils before they step into one help the constructiveness of the meeting? You decide!

1. *But we've always done it this way.* Dad's rule of thumb was that if you have been doing something for five years or more, you should take a look at it; it may be outdated.
2. *We tried it once and it didn't work.* Could the timing have been wrong? How about that all important factor, the execution of the idea? If that approach were taken, none of us would have learned to walk! Mr. Edison would have given up quickly on the light bulb. He tested thousands of materials for the filament (he was learning what did not work).
3. *Sure, it's a savings, but what about quality?* A knee-jerk reaction to trying something new. Perfect the quality as you put in the new.

4. *What's the use of saving half a person?* Halves can add up quickly. Savings can be real.
5. *It's not in the budget.* Flexibility is key in today's fast-moving world. Let's change the budget and build the business.
6. *Sure, but when will I have time?* This gets to the wonderful principle, "Don't do things right, do the right things." The key to success is the correct priorities. Take the time if it is worth it.
7. *They (the board, investors, etc.) would never let us do it.* Resell and retry repeatedly. Improve the idea, and your communication of it.

*All progress depends on the unreasonable man. The reasonable man adapts himself to the world. The unreasonable man persists in trying to adapt the world to himself.*
—George Bernard Shaw (1856–1950),
playwright, 1925 Nobel Prize winner

# 58 Listening and Learning: Why Silence Is a Valuable Skill

*I value the mute button on my phone, which silences my side of a conversation. No, it's not because I am talking behind someone's back, but because I know that there is no point in me talking with the mute button is on; this compels me to listen better. (I still find myself talking, then gratefully remember the mute is on!)*

Listening is a discipline, and not an easy one! When I'm speaking, I'm learning nothing. I'm not always learning even when listening, but I have a better chance.

I've found that it's much easier to keep myself quiet on the telephone when I have the help of my mute button. But I'm one who still believes that the best meetings are done person-to-person, eyeball-to-eyeball. Without my telephone mute button, I have had to develop my own internal mute button. (Some still think I could use it more.)

Over time I've found that it works best for me when I rest my hand over my mouth while I listen. This way I remind myself to let the speaker take center stage and for me to sit back and learn. (My very personal message to me is, "Shut up!") One of my former students actually pushes a thumbtack in his leg to remind himself to hold his tongue. Until I am able to surgically implant a mute button on my body I will continue to use my system. It has been helpful in enabling me to become a better listener.

Another big challenge for many folks, including yours truly, is that they become uncomfortable when silence occurs during a conversation and they feel compelled to fill in the quiet space. That's often a mistake. The individual across from you may be silently thinking of ways to express his thoughts better or may just be trying to recall something.

By filling in the silence, that is, "rescuing," you are actually interrupting and also diverting the conversation, as well as possibly suggesting a lack of interest in what the other person has to say. Let the other person talk. You will get the benefit of that person's best and most honest thoughts if you can keep yourself from jumping in and directing the conversation with your own agenda. In terms of communication skills, silence is priceless.

Here's an even bigger challenge! Instead of thinking up rebuttals to what the other person is saying, listen uncritically, seriously considering the potential correctness of the person's view. That way there is a better chance you will hear everything the person has to say on a given topic, and there is less chance of any misunderstandings.

---

### Mining for Diamonds

♦ "Shut up!" It's tough enough to shut up, and tougher still to really listen to another person. But work at it.
♦ Try turning on your mute button when talking on the telephone.
♦ Seriously consider that the other person has something valuable to share when he or she is speaking.

---

*Courage is what it takes to stand up and speak; courage is also what it takes to sit down and listen.*
—Sir Winston Churchill (1874–1965),
British Prime Minister

# 59 Mentors: Pro and Con

*In 1973 my wife and I attended a conference in Pebble Beach, California, where Ewing Marion Kauffman was the key speaker. He started Marion Laboratories in his basement and it developed into a company sold to Merrell Dow for $6.5 billion in 1989.*

*Over a drink after the presentation he invited me to drop by the office when I got home. This was the start of a 20-year relationship that lasted until he passed away in 1993. He shared every possible resource with me and when he did not feel he was the best person to give me answers or information, he steered me to those who could.*

*He would repeatedly ask me "Do you know why I keep working with you?" He would then explain that because we took his advice and used some he was pleased to continue; otherwise we were both wasting each other's time.*

A major part of Helzberg Diamonds' success was because of the extreme value of my mentors and the extreme openmindedness of my associates. Some companies suffer from the NIH syndrome (not invented here). They actually resent outsider's suggestions. In contrast, after a session with Mr. K, as he was known, my associates would sit me down and ask what I learned.

My personal vision of mentoring is that *no* individual advice will necessarily fit you. I see mentoring as a process of brain marination. When your brain is adequately marinated, you will look in the mirror and a light bulb on top of your cranium will flash the answer that best fits *you* and *your* situation. It may be a combination of your thoughts and some you received from your mentors. Some people would call it the work of your subconscious. Marination happens. Give it time. Don't force the issue.

In dealing with your mentors, listen, don't be defensive, and let them put forth every thought they have (push your mute button—see Hint 58). Use the time for *them* to talk, and do not tell them you've "tried that once" (see Hint 57). Shush!

In spite of growing up in a family where business was discussed on a nightly basis at the dinner table, I realize how much I *still* needed mentors. Mentors have made such major differences in my life in so many ways that I am a great believer.

The other side of the coin is that mentors are not for everyone. In Ray Smilor's book *Daring Visionaries: How Entrepreneurs Build Companies, Inspire Allegiance and Create Wealth*, he points out that "Some entrepreneurs prefer not to answer to someone else, to set their own work schedules and make their own mistakes because they are internally rather than externally directed. Successful entrepreneurs take personal responsibility for their success and perform best in situations where they have personal responsibility for results."

I have previously urged others to have an advisory board and mentors because that worked for me. I now realize "one size does not fit all" and urging all entrepreneurs to have mentors and advisory boards is not correct. Obviously, having an advisory board may not make you a greater entrepreneur. As my son, Barnett, at age 12, told me as I scripted him while he was on the telephone, "Dad, everyone has their own style!" Only you can decide your own style.

If you do choose to have a mentor, the prompter the thanks after your meeting the better. In a perfect world you will go by the post office on the way out of the mentor's office to mail the thank-you note. Following your meeting, it is key to give feedback to the mentor regarding the things you discussed, including the items you did and did not do, the whys and wherefores, and the success of those items you tried.

---

### Mining for Diamonds

♦ Find your mentors, develop relationships, and enjoy them.
♦ Most people love helping others. Ask them. (It's highly complimentary.)
♦ Don't use mentors or an advisory board if the techniques don't fit you! There is no crime in being the Lone Ranger.
♦ Thank your mentor immediately.
♦ Give your mentor prompt feedback on the topics discussed.
♦ Pass it on—help others.

---

*Just the discipline of having to put your thoughts in order with somebody else is a very useful thing.*
                    —Charles Munger, vice chairman,
                    Berkshire Hathaway

# 60 Building and Retaining Your Credibility

*I was the speaker at a community meeting in the days when diamonds were being touted as investments by some promoters in the "investment diamond business." When asked about diamonds as an investment, I explained that this was a misleading scam. I explained that legitimate jewelers were not selling diamonds for investment and that these were boiler-room sales operations that sold pork belly futures one week and diamonds the next. I also explained that no matter how reasonably one bought a diamond, he or she would not even get the wholesale value when selling since a buyer, professional or not, would be looking for a "steal" from an individual. I could tell my audience was somewhat surprised and that the credibility factor was tremendously reinforced when the audience heard the unexpected.*

Events such as those at Enron and Tyco create an atmosphere in which scrupulous honesty will be more valued than ever. A real plus for associates and customers will be putting a high value on honesty within the company. This creates a tremendous opportunity for the entrepreneur to build on a bedrock of honesty. This philosophy must include giving your associates as much disclosure and updating as can be done without divulging that which should be confidential. That includes giving employees, customers, and suppliers bad news before they hear extremely exaggerated and erroneous rumors from others. Who do you prefer managing damage control—you or your enemies?

Even if you are a charter member of America's Most Wanted Criminals, if you desire long-term profit you must operate on an ethical basis. An ethical basis means you must be up-front and consistent. One misstep after a thousand right steps will still be highly damaging.

Basically, it goes back to the philosophy, "Treat people as you want to be treated." That means you know what is omission and what is commission and to avoid both. What it *doesn't* mean is that you have to publicize things that can damage the company because they are confidential. What it *does* mean is that your communication should be as complete as possible at *every* level. My parents said it a little differently. "If they will steal for you, they will steal from you." You cannot play the two-faced game with customers without expecting your associates to play it with you. Consistency must include all parties.

One lesson I learned from my associates was that the more open management could be with the team members of the business, the more appreciation there was of the company and the more psychological *ownership* it gave others.

The less people are surprised and the more they can know things first without hearing it from others, the greater the pride and sense of ownership they will have in the business. Before that lousy earnings statement comes out, go to your banker. Tell her or him what is coming and why. Be proactive. Avoid surprises and omission like the proverbial plague. If bad news is coming it is far better for you to transmit it to associates, suppliers, and bankers than for the rumor mill to take over.

## Mining for Diamonds

♦ Guard your credibility zealously. Never, never, never abuse others' trust in you or your position.
♦ Deliver bad news *before* they hear it from others. Proactivity is key.
♦ Omission can be as damaging as commission.
♦ Never, never be manipulative.
♦ When news is bad, avoid surprises—warn those concerned.

*In looking for people to hire, you look for three qualities: integrity, intelligence, and energy. And if they don't have the first, the other two will kill you.*

—Warren Buffet, CEO,
Berkshire Hathaway

**61** ## The Question Is Not, "Are You Teaching?" The Question Is, "What Are You Teaching?"

*One day I followed the manager of the Prairie Village, Kansas, Bagel & Bagel restaurant in at 5:59 A.M. (opening time was 6:00 A.M.) and he screamed to his staff, "He got in!"*

*I once visited an auto dealership service department. Two gentlemen, both employed by the dealership, continued talking as I sat in my car. Actually, one looked at me like I was a Martian. I finally appealed that I needed service and only then did one of them schedule my maintenance.*

*I then went into the new car showroom at the same dealership. Although a number of individuals who seemed to be with the firm were in the showroom, no one approached me. I did manage to get someone to talk to me by walking out. Although I admire consistency, the actions of the service department and the sales department were definitely not service-oriented.*

Were these folks teaching? Absolutely! They clearly communicated that I as a customer, was an unwelcome interloper and a real interruption of other preferred tasks or nontasks! They were teaching their associates as well as the potential customer.

*Everything* you do communicates! You always set an example whether or not you want to! This is wonderful on days when you are excited and enthusiastic! On other days, your mood or actions might not be so wonderful, and you certainly would not like to see your associates or family feel or conduct themselves like you.

What is the entrepreneur who takes unfair advantage of his business for personal expenses teaching? In addition to providing certain employees with the power to send him to jail, as well as the attendant loss of reputation for his family, he is destroying associates' interest in saving a few cents on an office supply for the company.

There is a perception that if the boss does it, it is acceptable! Whatever you do, you are *teaching*. That is a great plus; it can also be a great minus if you don't keep it in mind and conduct yourself as you expect others to.

---

### Mining for Diamonds

♦ You are *always* teaching!
♦ The question is, "What are you teaching?"
♦ There are great teaching and learning opportunities when you are with your associates.
♦ You are always on stage. Treat customers and associates as you would have others treat them.

---

*An atmosphere encouraging exemplary behavior is probably even more important than rules, necessary though they are. During my tenure as chairman, I will consider myself the firm's chief compliance officer, and I have asked all 9,000 of Salomon's employees to assist me in that effort. I have also urged them to be guided by a test that goes beyond rules. Contemplating any business act, an employee should ask himself whether he would be willing to see it immediately described by an informed and critical reporter on the front page of his local paper, there to be read by his spouse, children, and friends. At Salomon, we simply want no part of any activities that pass legal tests but that we, as citizens would find offensive.*

> —Warren Buffett, investor
> Salomon Inc.: A Report by the Chairman on the Company's Standing and Outlook. *The New York Times*, Thursday, October 29, 1991

*In the arena of human life the honors and rewards fall to those who show their good qualities in action.*

> —Aristotle (384–322 B.C.E.), Greek philosopher

# 62 Dignifying Every Task: How to Win Your Associates' Commitment and Use Their Expertise

*When a young Charles Percy (later Senator Percy) was the head of Bell and Howell (a maker of fine cameras at that time), he increased productivity to an amazing extent. When asked how he did it, he said he used the "Wheelbarrow Story."*

*Percy explained that he did not believe in merely telling a worker in the factory to wheelbarrow needed parts to the other side of the plant. His philosophy was that the worker would perform the task better and more willingly if his supervisor took the time to explain the task's importance to the success of the entire plant. For example, the production line depends on wheelbarrowing those parts to the right place at the right time. "Production shuts down without your efforts."*

*Another true example, this time of how to discourage associates from buying into an operation's success. A consultant asked the manager of an incredibly expensive new warehouse, "Were you consulted on the new design? How is it working?" To which the manager replied, "It's a disaster! The big shots built it with the advice of some egghead consultant who came in from out of town."*

*Do you think this individual will go out of his way to prove the new warehouse works? I don't think so.*

The truth is that you often have access to top-quality talent and insightful advice nearer than you might think. Percy knew that when people feel valued and see that their efforts and ideas count for something, they will strive for peak performance.

Likewise, people who perform a job every day are just as much experts, and often more so, than consultants who live hundreds of miles away. Engage them in coming up with ways to improve the productivity of your business, using some of their ideas will commit them to the task much more readily than if you just tell them what to do.

Yes, there are diamonds buried in your own backyard! By asking for the opinions of associates, you immediately dignify the jobs they do, enhance their self-esteem, and increase their effectiveness. The manager in the warehouse example could surely have offered the designers of the new facility some inventive and practical ideas. In the process he would have likely developed a desire to help in debugging the plans before the new plant was built, thus ensuring its success. He also would have been far more interested in proving it worked after completion.

It's only natural that when you take time to explain the value of the work you are asking people to do they will feel motivated to do it better. By the same token, asking their opinions on how to simplify tasks can encourage them to find ways to be more effective. If you listen to their answers, you will reap tremendous dividends in higher morale and improved productivity.

## Mining for Diamonds

♦ Explaining to an associate why his or her job is important to the overall success of the business shows respect for the individual and the job.

♦ Ask associates how they would make their jobs more effective.

♦ Listen and change when proper.

♦ Discuss and explain if you do not change.

♦ Provide your associates with a sense of ownership over the jobs and tasks they are asked to perform.

*Human dignity is more precious than prestige.*
                    —Clause McKay (1890–1948), poet

*He that respects not is not respected.*
                    —George Herbert (1593–1633), poet

# 63 Asking: The Best Communication

*"Do you have mustard?" "Do you have plain vinegar?"*
*"Can I get more Diet Coke?" After 39 years of traveling*
*and eating in many restaurants, one day I suddenly real-*
*ized a simple fact: A question needs an answer! No*
*matter how simple the request, I found I could frame it*
*as a question. This was a far more effective way to com-*
*municate then telling the waitress I wanted mustard or*
*vinegar. (Many times my requests had gone unfilled.)*

I found this far more efficient and far more successful than the usual means of requesting food or service. I find the questioning technique very valuable in communication for that reason—it requires a response.

---

### Mining for Diamonds

♦ Ask! Don't tell!

---

*The smart ones ask when they don't know. And, sometimes,*
*when they do.* —Malcolm Forbes (1919–1990),
American publisher

*I had six honest men—they taught me all I knew: Their names*
*were Where and What and When—and Why and How and Who.*
—Rudyard Kipling (1865–1936),
author and poet

# 64 Negotiating: Learn It or Delegate It

*After asking Ted Cohn to be an advisory director at Helzberg Diamonds, I asked him how much he felt he should be compensated in this capacity. I thought we would negotiate his compensation, but before price was discussed I told him that regardless of what figure he named he would be getting cheated. That is how I felt about his talent and brilliance.*

Although I resent arrogance terribly, I have long made the claim to be the worst negotiator in the United States. I don't believe that's arrogant. It would be if I claimed to be the worst negotiator in the world. I think it is really important to know your own negotiating abilities. Some people are trainable and some are not. (I am not.)

Why is this chapter here if I cannot help you negotiate better?

- To influence you to use others to negotiate if you are the wrong person.
- To tell you that good negotiating training courses are available.
- To tell you the only thing I know about negotiating—smart is dumb, dumb is smart.

**Mining for Diamonds**

♦ You may not be a negotiator! Let others more skilled do it.
♦ Good resources exist in negotiation training.
♦ Smart is dumb; dumb is smart.

*Never seem wiser or more learned than the company you are with.*
*Treat your learning like a watch and keep it hidden. Do not pull it*
*out to count the hours, but give the time when you are asked.*
                                        —Lord Chesterfield (1694–1773),
                                        English politician

**65** ## In Marketing, Don't Say It—Be It

I *was in California participating in a seminar for the International Council of Shopping Centers when I heard about a ready-to-wear store that had signs inviting people in with their food and drink. Nearly all retail stores display signs asking folks not to bring in food and drink. I was intrigued, as here was a store that made it clear to the potential customer that the store was there to serve on the customer's terms, not the store owners'.*

*In the world of marketing, in which so many establishments claim that they are friendly and then create such negative rules, this looked like an example of truly being friendly, not just saying they are friendly. So we immediately copied the idea and put up signs in all Helzberg stores inviting passersby in with their food and drink. We felt it clearly communicated the message that we were different from other stores.*

*The interesting part was that when people saw the words "food and drink" they would stand outside the stores to finish their ice cream cones. When we saw this happening, we would walk over to encourage potential customers to bring their food inside and jokingly tell them they were especially welcome if they shared!*

*Adding to the fun, Carousel Snack Bars put up signs that said, "You are welcome to show off your Helzberg Diamonds while enjoying your food and drink."*

Our sign was a conversation starter and a mood creator, and we believed it communicated loudly and clearly why we were there—to serve customers on their terms! Folks were careful with their goodies and rarely was additional work created by carelessness or messiness. I am totally mystified by the no-food-and-drink signs abounding in stores, given the millions of dollars spent in advertising and promotion enticing people to visit retail stores every year. Here is a nearly cost-free method to welcome customers rather than telling them to stay out.

I ask my ready-to-wear friends, "Is damage to one or two dresses a year worth the cost to get more guests in your store?" Talk about risk and reward ratios! Obviously, I just didn't get it!

Are you doing anything in your business to turn off customers? Is there a standard industry practice that might give you the opportunity to differentiate yourself from others by doing the opposite?

---

### Mining for Diamonds

♦ Don't say you are friendly. Be friendly.
♦ First, make them comfortable.
♦ Second, make a friend.
♦ Third, make a customer.
♦ If you don't make a customer, make a friend!
♦ Don't make claims that are not deliverable.

---

*Separate checks anytime you ask . . . just give us a couple of extra minutes.*
*No extra charge if you share or ask for an extra plate.*
*Special requests are not a problem. "If we can, we will."*
*We never charge an automatic gratuity for any size party.*
                        —First Watch Restaurant menu, Fairway, Kansas

**66** **Preparing for Controversial Meetings**

*The coming meeting of the board of the not-for-profit organization was to handle the most controversial possible issue, the conversion of a boys' school to a co-educational school. As chairman, I visited with each member of the board individually, getting their thoughts and feelings and sharing the potential direction of the institution. This turned out to be very helpful in terms of getting everyone's feelings privately to see if the change was feasible. It gave me the chance to explain the reasons for considering change and reasons to consider it in a positive light. The board voted unanimously for the motion without an undue amount of time and discussion. Apparently, I had unconsciously done the right thing.*

The individual visits created opportunities to learn the feelings of each member without the presence of other board members. It also gave the board members the opportunity to talk privately about their feelings about the matter. The visit gave me the opportunity to learn things that I did not know or had not properly considered, as well as to learn potential objections.

It also avoided letting any individual members paint themself into a corner by stating their feelings very strongly in one direction in a group setting and being embarrassed to change. It also gave members the courtesy of showing respect for their opinions and thoughts. It added to my body of knowledge as well as allowing me to discuss their hopes, dreams, and fears for the institution.

### Mining for Diamonds

♦ Investing time in advance of a meeting with individuals one-on-one pays when warranted by the gravity of the decision.
♦ This enables those who do not always state all their concerns in a meeting to do so in private.
♦ It gives you a chance to convince others who may be on the fence or opposed to the change.
♦ It will avoid a confrontational meeting if your goal is incorrect, unattainable, or poorly timed.

*The people to fear are not those who disagree with you, but those who disagree with you and are too cowardly to let you know.*
—Napoleon Bonaparte (1769–1821),
soldier, emperor, statesman

# 67 Shortening Those Damn Meetings and Making Them More Effective!

*One bright day I observed myself in a meeting of the board of a business incubator. My right hand was up! There I was, voting for something about which I had originally been very negative. At home that night I looked in the mirror and asked myself, "Why didn't you bore the board with your long diatribe about why you were against the motion and why did you vote for it? What changed your mind?"*

*The answer is that prior to the board meeting the people who called the meeting prepared a very detailed question-and-answer sheet for participants. The sheet addressed the pros and cons; even the difficult, nasty questions were included and carefully written answers explained both sides of each facet of the potential decision. I entered the meeting convinced that my original posture on the question was not correct. No time was wasted with my diatribe. I voted for rather than against the motion.*

*Later I saw the ultimate version of this technique used by the Jewish Heritage Foundation of Kansas City. A sheet was created for each of the 10 topics to be considered at the six-hour meeting scheduled on a Sunday. Each sheet listed the present policy or practice to be addressed, the potential change in policy, and the pluses and minuses of each potential change to be considered.*

*All attendees received the document in advance of the meeting, giving them a chance to think about the pluses and minuses of each proposal. It also gave them a chance to think of any plus or minus not listed that they could address at the meeting. Result: A highly informed, educated board learned a great deal and the highly productive meeting with concrete results took less than one-half of the time allotted.*

The result was to save a tremendous amount of time and end up with wise decisions and to create a base of understanding that encouraged prior thinking and familiarity so only intelligent non-time-wasting questions came up. Borrowing this technique has created the same advantages for other organizations.

Here is an Example:

Should we monitor grants beyond current practice? How deep should the process go? How intrusive/demanding should we be? Does the monitoring process imply future funding? Should grants be linked to program outcomes?

- **Present Foundation Policy or Practice:**
  The Foundation utilizes a variety of monitoring techniques which include: a written progress report every 6 months until all Foundation funds have been expended; on-site staff visits; on-site staff and Board visits; Foundation office visits; telephone inquiries about grant progress; a review of canceled grant checks; conversations with other funders; street talk.

- **Possible Modifications of Present Foundation Policy or Practice:**
  - Increase the level and scope of monitoring.
  - Decrease the level and scope of monitoring,

- **Points to Consider in Favor of Increasing the Level and Scope of Monitoring:**
  - With more knowledge about agency progress, the Foundation could offer more assistance to agencies and have better data with which to make future funding.
  - Probabilities of being unaware of grants whose outcomes are not satisfactory would be decreased.
  - Increase Board's participation in all aspects of grant making while increasing their knowledge of agency operations.

- **Points to Consider in Opposition of Increasing the Level and Scope of Monitoring:**
  - Increased staff and Board time utilization.
  - The Foundation may be perceived as becoming too instrusive in the agency's operations (always a delicate balance).
  - Increased monitoring may send an incorrect signal to the agency that future funding will be granted.

- **Points to Consider in Favor of Decreasing the Level and Scope of Monitoring:**
  - Less expenditure of staff and board time in monitoring activities.
  - Less agency time spent in meeting Foundation monitoring request.

- **Points to Consider in Opposition of Decreasing the Level and Scope of Monitoring:**
  - Foundation's ability to exercise stewardship over grants is diminished.
  - A decreased knowledge base of past agency activity makes future funding decisions more difficult and less certain.

---

**Mining for Diamonds**

♦ The more effort you put in before the meeting, the better chance for quality resolution and time savings.
♦ If you want to cut meeting time and increase effectiveness, try this approach.

---

*If you had to identify, in one word the reason why the human race has not achieved its' full potential, that word would be "meetings"!*

—Dave Barry, author, humor columnist,
1988 Pulitizer Prize winner

# 68 Marty Ross's Magic Follow-Up System

*In 1970 I had the privilege of starting a seven-year stint working with a fine individual and outstanding professional manager named Marty Ross. Marty saw himself as a teacher rather than a manager. Teach us he did! One of his many gems was his follow-up system. He would mark a date on a reminder note he wanted to revisit with the words "follow up" and then file it in his follow-up file for that month, date, and year. This was not a procrastination tool, but a highly visual reminder system.*

*His yearly follow-up file consisted of 12 monthly folders, 31 daily folders, and future year folders. Initially, he put items in the monthly folders and at the beginning of each month put those follow-up items into the file for the day when he wanted to see it.*

*This works for two-week follow-up, for the annual Christmas, birthday, or anniversary follow-up, or for the five-year follow-up. It also reminds you to follow up on the assigned projects of other associates, making you a better executive and freeing you from trying to carry innumerable details in your mind. Marty actually prided himself on not needing to remember things and not cluttering up his mind. This is not instead of, but in addition to, a day planner.*

*For an entrepreneur giving assignments to individuals this can remind you when to follow up with team members. He also kept a file for each direct report of his to review what to discuss with each individual at their weekly meeting.*

One additional way I use this system is that when I view a classic article I wish to reread annually, I put it in follow-up for one year later instead of consigning it to a file where it will be forgotten. It is handy for vital items such as renewal reminders on trademarks, where I put the reminder in follow-up for three different days. I did experience a law firm allowing one trademark to lapse, an unforgivable flaw in their follow-up system.

Marty's system has been priceless to me for over 30 years. Unfortunately, Marty passed away at the age of 53. His personal follow-ups sustained the systems he created, as he knew they would.

---

### Mining for Diamonds

- A follow-up system is invaluable and priceless.
- Consider using it for reminders and classic items you wish to share and/or review annually.
- Single pieces of paper or lengthy documents work in this system.
- Put in three follow-ups for three different dates on do-or-die items like lease expirations or trademark renewals.
- Take the onus off yourself as far as trying to remember things. Build the system to do it.

*The young man who addresses himself in stern earnest to organizing his life—his habits, his associations, his reading, his study, his work—stands far more chance of rising to a position affording him opportunity to exercise his organizing abilities than the fellow who dawdles along without chart or compass, without plan or purpose, without self-improvement and self-discipline.*

—B. C. Forbes (1880–1954),
publisher, founder *Forbes* magazine

**69** ## Your Struggle to Get Honest Feedback

*Our controller quit, explaining that he did not feel this was the right type of job for him. He was going on to more intellectual pursuits. Subsequently, one of our vice presidents told me he had not thought the controller fit the job. When I asked why he did not tell me before, he explained, "I thought you liked him."*

*This was painful to me, a guy who thought he had made people comfortable in stating their thoughts, opinions, and perceptions openly. It made me recall the Hans Christian Andersen story of the emperor who wore no clothes yet no one would tell him he was stark naked.*

*Consider the possibility that you are the emperor, that you may not know some very vital things about the business that you should know. Do your associates feel they would offend you if they told you things that do not agree with your perceptions or desires?*

If you are genuinely interested in honest feedback, you have a tremendous challenge before you. Here are some far from foolproof methods of getting thoughts and suggestions and getting started in the right direction.

Asking questions is key. It must be clear that you are fishing for help and constructive comments and not compliments or the "right" answers. Yes, positives tell you what to continue, but they usually come in due time, and don't help you progress.

If honest feedback is something you want, please know *how* difficult it is to get! My frustration has brought me to tell my students, "I like compliments, but they *don't* help improve this course. How can this course be improved?" (Note lack of "I"; thus they are not insulting nor hurting me!) By asking this question of my MBA students at Rockhurst University, I have received priceless advice. I admit I do some begging, explaining that the classes before them made the course better for them so they need to help improve the course for the sake of future students.

Focus the question on exactly what you want to know. That makes individuals comfortable to communicate something they might normally feel is negative or is something they believe you would rather not hear.

The three magic questions were brought to my class by a highly accomplished guest speaker named Mary McElroy. Students were complaining that their annual salary reviews were only pats on the head accompanied by raises, but gave them no guidance on how to improve their performance or progress in their careers. Her answer: Ask the three magic questions:

1. What am I doing that you like?
2. What am I doing that you do not like?
3. What am I not doing that you would like?

These questions can be answered at annual reviews even if not asked by the person being reviewed, I know of companies asking them of customers and getting valuable feedback. It may improve your level of communication tremendously.

If you are not interested in hearing the unvarnished truth, by all means, do not ask. That is manipulation, a most negative procedure that is counterproductive and fools no one.

## Mining for Diamonds

- If you really want honest feedback, you must perfect your own techniques for getting it. Ask the right (highly focused) questions.
- Customize the three magic questions for any particular use:
  - ◊ What do you like that is happening?
  - ◊ What don't you like that is happening?
  - ◊ What would you like that is not happening?
- Ask, "How do we improve?"
- Listen! Listen! Listen!
- You must consistently prove through verbal and nonverbal signals that you want the story as others see it.
- Write thoughts down and respond, after due thought and consideration. Do not give quick, immediate answers unless appropriate.
- One negative vibe from you when getting honest feedback that is not the most pleasing will echo through the organization. You must desperately want this information.

*If people are not being told the truth about their problems, the majority not only may, but invariably must, make the wrong judgments.*

*—Ralph Ingersoll, editor and publisher*

# 70 To Lunch or Not to Lunch with Your Client, Supplier, or Associate

*Our landlord had previously refused to let us vacate our store and discontinue running it. I took him to lunch and we had a nice conversation which enhanced our relationship. Years later I took him to lunch again and after a meal and a couple of drinks remade my pitch about vacating the store. This time, after a full discussion, he agreed to let us close down. Our relationship continued to be extremely cordial, if not more so, after that lunch.*

Is it always smart to take your client or supplier (prospective or actual) to lunch or breakfast? No! Use your judgment.

If you want to build up the relationship, especially in the early stage, it probably is a good strategy. If you want to avoid being Ms. Nice or Mr. Nice, that is, in some negotiation situations, avoid dining together.

Think it out. What is your goal and what is your purpose? If a touchy-feely relationship is counterproductive to your goal, don't break bread.

### Mining for Diamonds

♦ Think it out before you dine.
♦ Don't dine when a less personal relationship is more appropriate.

*Closeness and friendship are impediments to sound business deals.*                    —Shmarya Levin, co-worker of Henzl

# 71 Avoid Those Buzzwords and Alphabet Soup

*As I sat in the board meeting listening to the board president, my mind wandered as I tried to translate the alphabet soup he kept serving—MAMTEC then KTEC, one acronym after another. I became lost in the mind-numbing array of undecipherables and heard little of the presentation. I felt rather stupid drowning in acronym soup, believing I was the only dummy in the room until one board member finally piped up and asked for translations.*

If you wish to select automatic turnoff buttons when selling ideas, two quick ways to lose your audience are by using buzzwords and alphabet soup acronyms. Buzzwords, even when decipherable, can be troublesome to some, distracting or demeaning to others, and sometimes make the speaker look slick.

Admittedly, some are extremely useful. My personal favorite is "in a perfect world," which embodies what I am trying to communicate in this hint. I am quite unsure what a "strategic initiative" is or for that matter "leading lipstick indicators" or "process." Surely, you get the idea. Ask your computer's search engine for buzzwords for a more complete list.

Turning off listeners will not win battles. It will lose wars.

## Mining for Diamonds

♦ Don't do things that put others down! Don't use acronyms or fancy words they don't know.
♦ Don't try to look smarter than anyone in the room.
♦ Remember, "Smart is dumb, dumb is smart!"
♦ Opinion: Avoid "as it were" and "if you will," which are meaningless except to show how intellectual you are.

*Buzzwords: The verbal equivalent of dressing for success in the business world, where a vocabulary that includes leveraging or incremental will lift your status as surely as a power suit or corporate suspenders.*

—Rick Bayan, author of *The Cynic's Dictionary*

# Helzberg Hint 72 — Should You Communicate Your Success?

*Dad was the ultimate extrovert, yet he told me that the right strategy was to be a "sleeper," that is, not to be known for success when it did come. Interestingly, this thought was confirmed by Leonard Lauder of Estée Lauder, who told an audience of entrepreneurs, "Don't communicate your success—others will steal your people and your ideas."*

*At one point our buyers got very unhappy with me; in spite of the success of the company, they would visit potential suppliers who had never heard of us! As your business becomes more and more successful, you will inevitably be asked to speak at meetings, interview for articles, and generally do certain things that create a higher and higher profile for the business.*

There are pluses and minuses regarding the publicity you may garner (one minus is the old rule that being on the cover of *Time* magazine is the kiss of death). Consider the pluses and minuses carefully. Assume everything you share will be placed in the spot where you least desire it, and conduct yourself accordingly. That will help avoid any regrets later.

## Mining for Diamonds

♦ Think out carefully opportunities for publicity that disclose anything about the company you do not wish your number one competitor to know.

♦ Control carefully the information that goes outside the company and even the information that does not.

♦ As you grow, realize that a little paranoia is a healthy thing; share what benefits the company.

♦ Realize that a higher profile creates more scrutiny of what you do.

♦ Understand the differing implications of local and industry publicity. Local may help your sales if your market is local, whereas industry publicity may just help your ego.

♦ If your ego is the problem, recognize it and contain yourself.

*Don't communicate your success—they will steal your people and your ideas.*

—Leonard Lauder, chairman of
The Estée Lauder Companies Inc.

*Be a sleeper.*                          —B. C. Helzberg, Sr.

# 73 Avoiding the Use of "I"— and Using It Properly

*When unhappy with someone's behavior or perform-ance, that is the time to start with "I." "I'm disap-pointed," "I'm upset," Not "You messed up," "You are lazy," or "You are stupid." Never attack anyone's self-respect. Further, talk about the situation, not about the personality.*

One must be judicious in how and when "I" is used. Remem-bering that others are far more interested in *themselves* than you is a winning strategy.

On the other hand "I" is appropriate when you are not in agreement as in "I don't understand." Avoid "I disagree" which usually guarantees a barrier to communication. When you dis-agree, it can be effective and courteous to say, "I'm really strug-gling with this idea or that conclusion. Please explain it further."

The other appropriate time to use "I" is when taking re-sponsibility for failure to perform. This only gains respect and saves the time-wasting investigation of who is to blame, a non-productive exercise at best.

---

### Mining for Diamonds

- Remember that others are far more interested in themselves than in you.
- It is more effective to say, "I am disappointed" than "you messed up."
- Use "I" to take responsibility for your own failure or lack of understanding.

---

*Ego: A helium-filled balloon that often lifts the ambitious to lofty destinations, where the change in pressure can cause it to pop unexpectedly.*
— Rick Bayan, author of *The Cynic's Dictionary*

*The bigger a man's head gets, the easier it is to fill his shoes.*
— Henry A. Courtney (1916–1945),
war hero, recipient of Medal of Honor

*Even Inspector Clouseau could find last year's guilty party: your Chairman. My performance reminds me of the quarterback whose report card showed four F's and a D but who nonetheless had an understanding coach. "Son," he drawled, "I think you're spending too much time on that one subject."*
— Warren Buffett, investor,
Berkshire Hathaway Annual Report 1999

# 74 No Surprises

*The "no surprises" principle of usage in good communication has been well demonstrated by Alan Greenspan. The newspapers were saying that prior to the Fed's early fall 1999 increase in interest rates that he had "done everything but jump up and down and say the rate will be raised."*

*As a consequence, it was no surprise to the market or the financial community when interest rates actually did rise from 5.25 to 5.50 percent. Life went on normally because everyone expected the rise, although they did not know the size of it in advance.*

Greenspan is a great role model. There is no horrible shock factor in your actions when you have properly telegraphed in advance what could or might happen, that is, planted the seeds. Thus, you may be able to avoid a firestorm when the change comes if you have preconditioned the audience. In the excellent book *First, Break All the Rules!* the authors tell how much more positively nurses administering hypodermic shots were perceived who warned the patient, "This will hurt a little" than the ones who said, "It won't hurt a bit"—the better nurses preconditioned the patients for the shock. If you can precondition your team for the possibility that the change might come some day, it will avoid the surprise factor when practical to do so.

Furthermore, to avoid the shock, especially when news is bad, it is always far better to hear it first from the boss rather than from third-hand exaggerated reports and rumors from others. This especially applies to your bankers and your associates.

When you can practically and comfortably talk about the possibility of something happening in advance, you will do well to heed Alan Greenspan's example. This relates to urgency as well as substance. Bad news does travel faster than the speed of light, and you *must* get ahead of the rumor mill to avoid the inevitable problems that follow trumped-up rumors.

An example of poor management practice is when an employee is actually surprised when fired.

---

### Mining for Diamonds

♦ Avoid surprises when at all possible. You will avoid lots of problems. It's fairer to your associates, family, and friends! You'll have to deal with far less shock and potential disappointment and upset.

♦ You will find an amazing appreciation and acceptance when you explain bad news to others if they hear it first from you.

---

*The best defense is a good offense.*

—B. C. Helzberg, Sr.

# 75 Care and Feeding of Your Associates

*Prior to opening a new store, we would conduct train-*
*ing seminars; I had the honor of being one of the presen-*
*ters. This gave me a chance to meet new associates and*
*strengthen my bonds with the old timers opening the*
*new shop. I had been asking, "Who is number one?" as*
*part of my presentation and, of course, the answer*
*seemed obvious—the customer. Everyone at the meeting*
*would loudly proclaim the answer.*

Then one day after about 30 years of experience, another in-
stant flash of the obvious; I suddenly realized that numero
uno was not the customer but our own associates; everything
literally emanated from them. They were the key to the success of
the company—without question. That means you treat each with
respect and you celebrate and glorify the success of the leaders
in performance.

I would so enjoy sending gifts to the top 25 salespeople each
month, including a model of a Mercedes with my handwritten
card explaining that we were the only jewelry firm buying a
Mercedes for the top sales producers.

Our honoring the top sales producers knew no bounds.
My wife and I would invite them to our home annually for the
predinner event, to be followed by an elaborate dinner in a fine
hotel, with all the show business glitz imaginable tied in with honoring each individual, including the band playing the tune for
each state or city of the recipient as each came to the podium for
his or her award.

Each fifth year we would take managers and spouses to a fine resort for a few days. With growth, the cost would have been so gigantic that cooler heads prevailed and we discontinued those trips.

The store managers were among the people to be treasured and when I visited, I would enjoy the one-to-one contact at lunch or dinner.

Mall hours really helped. It enabled me to cover many stores in a market in one or two days by starting at breakfast with a manager or all local associates, and then being able to visit open stores until 9 P.M. and possibly have a late meal with the manager afterwards.

The old song that says, "You gotta love 'em in the A.M., love 'em in the P.M." always comes to mind when I think about Helzberg associates.

What about a lack of success: a store has a red day because of a large return. I remember calling a manager and sympathizing with her after one of those. I did not repeat that call nearly enough.

My wife was observant of the way we treated our associates and would repeatedly chide me by saying "Treat me like I work for the company!" That showed me I was on the right track, at least with my associates.

---

### Mining for Diamonds

♦ Celebrate any kind of success of associates.
♦ Love 'em in the A.M., love 'em in the P.M.
♦ Use any excuse to write personal handwritten notes to associates: a new baby, a new hourse, etc. If you care, show it—that includes family losses and tragedies.
♦ Kiss them until their lips are chapped!

---

*Accept the fact that we have to treat almost anybody as a volunteer.*
—Peter Drucker, writer, educator,
management consultant

*I think the greatest thing that an executive, a leader, or a so-called manager must have is a caring relationship with people.*
—Ewing M. Kauffman (1916–1993),
pharmaceutical enterpreneur

*You do not lead by hitting people over the head—that's assault not leadership.*
—Dwight D. Eisenhower (1890–1969),
general and 34th U.S. President

# 76 Care and Feeding of Your Suppliers

*Lionel ran a mall shoe business much like many others. The method he used to get out in front of the competition was by having the newest styles earlier and in more profusion than the competition. How did he make this happen? A close relationship with his suppliers was his route to success. When salesmen came to his offices, they were immediately treated like important guests. They were invited in, given a cup of coffee, and then escorted to a special elevator "for our shoe suppliers" to make it easier for them to handle their heavy display cases. At quarterly shoe shows he would pick up the bar bills and meal bills. He even remembered their family member's birthdays. He simply treated them like his best customers rather than as suppliers.*

The results: who got the styles at the earliest times? Who got the shipments when there were shortages? Whose stores stood out in merchandising? Lionel's did.

*Another example: The Marion Laboratories team returned from Germany to tell Ewing Kauffman of the great deal they had negotiated with a new supplier of a pharmaceutical product. The purchasing agent then went to the original supplier who lowered his cost to keep their business. Kauffman asked his associate if the supplier they had successfully negotiated with could make any money on the contract. The answer was no. Kauffman had his team return to raise the agreed-to price so that the supplier could make a profit.*

When the only other supplier of this particular product later went out of business, Marion Laboratories was left with their good and friendly supplier.

The moral of the story is that there are some folks who became very successful by treating people, including those they buy from, the way they want to be treated.

---

### Mining for Diamonds

♦ A conscious decision should be made regarding treatment of suppliers.
♦ Your team should get together periodically to review your care and feeding program and its effectiveness.
♦ The program should be reviewed periodically for potential additions and deletions.
♦ You need to create an overall attitude in the company so there is consistency and conformity to your policy.

---

*Do unto others as they do unto you. Plus 10 percent.*
—Henry Kissinger, diplomat,
1973 Nobel Peace Prize recipient

# 77 Care and Feeding of Your Lenders

*Our company had borrowed $500,000 from the Prudential Insurance Company. We had gotten ourselves into a rut with the wrong direction and a notable lack of profits, lack of a decent balance sheet, and a lack of progress. Fred Kennedy and Dick Anderson, the Prudential representatives, would come to visit periodically. We had built up a good relationship over the years. When they visited us, things were not going well at all and much to our amazement they were highly supportive. The value of honest relationships was again confirmed.*

Your bankers and other lenders can be extremely important people to your long-term progress and success. Treating them as partners can pay huge dividends, enabling you to borrow more with fewer restrictions.

Basically, treat them as investors and partners. Underpromise and overdeliver. If they want quarterly statements, consider giving them monthly statements. If they want to meet annually at their office, invite them to yours. Schedule a walk through the plant, warehouse, or store and explain your plans; tell them what you see—right and wrong. Talk about contemplated changes to help them to see beyond the figures.

Let your key people make presentations to them, giving teammates ownership, showing those you are so proud of to the banks, and showing depth of management if you have it. Most of all, no surprises. If you know results will be poor for a period, let them be the first to know even before the exact figures are available. Warn them in advance of that statement, telling them the whys and wherefores, what you learned, and where you are going from here. The worst-case scenario is others hearing rumors of bad news before you tell them. The best defense is nearly always a good offense. Be proactive—it will pay dividends. Your lenders will gain a comfort level because of your integrity in financial reporting and keeping commitments of trust. Your lenders have excellent noses for odiferous situations made far sharper by Enron, Andersen, and Tyco.

Treat lenders like the treasures they can be for your future. Build a personal relationship at banks where that is an option. Consider avoiding the institutions where your loan applications are sent to a lifeless computer thousands of miles away for a verdict on your next loan. Deal with a human with decision-making responsibility.

The title of this book would have been far different if we had not had a longtime personal relationship with a great banker. Above all, do not wait for the lifeboat until you are drowning. Make friends with the captain now.

---

### Mining for Diamonds

- Nurture relationships with lenders well in advance of needs.
- Invite them to your shop and explain the business to them and your strategy for your company.
- Show them some weak spots you are working on as well as your strengths. "Negative selling" builds credibility unless you are perfect.
- Let your top teammates give brief presentations to the lenders.
- Never let lenders get unpleasant surprises about your company. Never.

---

*All virtue is summed up in dealing justly.*
                    —Aristotle (384–322 B.C.E.), Greek philosopher

# Part VI

## Focusing

# 78 What Business Are You Really In?

*When air travel began to grow more predominant in the mid-twentieth century, Canadian Pacific Railways was ready. The company had already defined its mission as providing transportation for people and cargo. It created Canadian Pacific Airlines!*

*Farther south, American railroads had defined their business as railroading—just railroading. They did not see their business as transportation. Not sensing that contributed to their downfall.*

Helzberg Diamonds' business is jewelry, not shopping malls. When we added freestanding stores to our operations, we did not change our type of business any more than we did when we left the downtowns for the malls. We still sold jewelry; we just sold it in a different setting. When Helzberg dropped many other lines of merchandise (even watches for some years), the store signs were changed to "Helzberg Diamonds" from "Helzberg Jewelers." We focused on who we wanted to be and how we wanted to be perceived.

In addition to knowing what business you are in, you need to *tell people* what business you are in. Your company name is extremely important, considering that consumers are hit with thousands of advertising messages every single day. I was proud of our company name because it told exactly what we were, and I tried to make it a religion that we would not say the word "Helzberg" without "Diamonds."

I am always confounded when the name of the company or the store does not portray what it is. What is "Joe's"? A successful restaurant, a clothing store, or a pipefitting company? Are there exceptions? Absolutely. This is one person's view. You need a name that portrays who you are and what you are. If you aren't Boeing or Clorox, maybe you should explain what you are.

Ask yourself, "What business am I really in?"

*The railroad business or the transportation business?*
*The movie business or the entertainment business?*
*The mall business or the retail business?*
*The food business or the hospitality business?*
*The photographic film business or the transfer-of-images business?*

What could be more challenging and exciting than the continuing changes of *the business world*? Fighting change is trying to hold off the inevitable. Change is going to occur, no matter what you do, so be prepared for the twists and turns in your industry. Don't be stuck in what has been, like so many of the downtown merchants who did not seize the earliest opportunities to open in covered malls (I know this firsthand because I was one).

When television first came out, the movie industry had a picnic making fun of what it perceived to be new competition. Broken-down televisions became part of movie scripts! The humor was sharp, pointed, and reactive. Today, the relationship, though perhaps not 100 percent symbiotic, is benefiting from the growth of television programming and of VCR and DVD usage.

The retail jewelry industry has gone through drastic changes as well. At one point in the distant past, optometrists rented space in credit jewelry stores. This arrangement helped profits and brought in new customers. When this arrangement was threatened, many retailers including me, lobbied legislators to prevent the demise of the optometrist in the retail stores. Actually, when optometrists discontinued operations in our stores the advantages included a far better focus. Change was inevitable. It was a waste of time, dollars, and focus to fruitlessly fight the inevitable!

I especially enjoyed the eight years we focused on diamonds when our jewelry stores carried no watches. This decision was not made in a 100 percent rational way. I unpacked watches for the opening of the Park Mall (now called Park Place) store in Tucson and repacked them, saying, "This will be the first Helzberg store never to sell a watch!" (Ah, the joys of entrepreneurship!) We had some very profitable years during that period. It appeared to me that 90 percent of all customer complaints had been emanating from 8 percent of our volume (i.e., watches). I felt we would rid ourselves of many headaches if all our associates focused solely on diamonds. To paraphrase Ford ("Does it sell Fords?"), my guiding question was, "Does it sell diamonds?" I also had the feeling that being somewhat different from the competition gave our associates some pride.

Being counterintuitive and having it work can be lots of fun. After my day in the sun, our new management put watches back into Helzberg stores, with which I had no quarrel. As Dad said, "There's your way, my way, and the right way!"

---

### Mining for Diamonds

♦ Focus! Focus! Focus!
♦ Less is more. (That's a promise!)
♦ Do what you do best. To heck with the rest.
♦ Use this test for your decisions: "Will this get us closer to our objective?" If it only makes money, it might be a mistake.

---

*We made a deal with the bank. They don't make pizzas. We don't take checks.* —Sign at Shakey's Pizza

*I don't know the key to success, but the key to failure is to try to please everyone.* —Bill Cosby, comedian, actor, author

# 79 Balancing Your Life . . . Work, Play, Children, Health, and Money

*It was the day of one of our great ice storms. I arrived at the office about 6:00 A.M. What was in my mind? Be an example and prove that you need not be late to work that day regardless of the weather? The workday started at 8:00 A.M. What earthly difference could I make in being two hours early?*

To some great extent, I got in the habit of overreacting because being the boss's son I wanted to prove I could work longer and harder than anyone else. Obviously, productivity is far more important than activity, but I confused one with the other. Based on things seen in other companies, I felt everyone expected me to be a bum and/or destroy the business.

I recall certain times when I could have taken more time with my family than I did and realize if I had come to treasure productivity more highly than activity, I would have done so. I also understand one of my great motivators was the fact that I was the boss's son and the intense motivation that gave me was valuable, but I could have used a little more balance. Working hard when being productive is certainly intelligent. Although I feel very fortunate in my relationships with my family, I was overly interested in input as opposed to output; the hours spent working mattered as well as sales and profits and building a business with great people.

The obvious fact that time with children is very limited at best did dawn on me along the way. We had some great family trips and fishing trips. I drove with them to college and back feeling like a very happy thief stealing one-to-one time with each. Most entrepreneurs I have known care a great deal about their families and give a good deal of thought to the implications of entrepreneurship. You need a highly supportive spouse and family, and the realization that you do not have unlimited control of your agenda, especially when a crisis arises.

Other parts of the balancing mix include health, which is affected and controlled to some great extent by you in the areas of weight, strength, and flexibility, although not in chronology. Is your most vigorous exercise on a golf cart?

What do you want to look back on when your children are adults—what memories and times with them? Are you committed to preserving your friendship and love with your spouse so when your children leave, two strangers will not be left at home?

I especially admire today's entrepreneurs because they consciously think about these parts of their lives in relation to their business decisions. I did not see this happening in my generation to an equal extent. Family implications are a major piece of your entrepreneurial decision. It goes much further because your family will have to deal with your emotions and financial strains when things are very difficult in the business. Your own reaction to these traumas is worth considering. It is well worth taking the time to decide your priorities and discuss the implications of entrepreneurship with your family.

## Mining for Diamonds

- Value output not input. Putting in unnecessary hours without results is foolish.
- Don't confuse activity with productivity.
- Balance your life. Treasure every moment with your family. The opportunities won't return.
- Have a supportive spouse who understands the time you need to take with the business and is a wonderful parent for your children.
- Are you taking care of your health properly? Are you a study in deferred maintenance?
- Your life as an entrepreneur is not in your total control; the family is affected by business crises and the business is affected by family crises. Expect crises, and prepare for them if possible. At least be aware of the inevitability of crises along the journey of life.

*I wish that I had known sooner that if you miss a child's play or performance or sporting event, you will have forgotten a year later the work emergency that caused you to miss it. But the child won't have forgotten that you weren't there.*
> —Laurel Culter, vice chairman, Foote, Cone & Belding

*To be happy at home is the ultimate result of ambition.*
> —Samuel Johnson (1740–1795),
> English poet, essayist, critic, journalist

*The cost of success will be too high if you choose not to lead a balanced life.*
> —Linda Stryker, missionary nurse

# 80 Giving Back

Giving back may be the most fun you will ever have. Giving back is the most selfish thing I do personally because I get so much out of it. I don't feel it's in any way generosity, but rather the most enjoyable, the most ennobling and perhaps the most selfish thing I do.

The other side of giving back is the example of individuals who for ego reasons take positions in charities when their companies and their employees are at risk for their jobs or their bonuses. Your first duty as an entrepreneur is to make your company profitable in order to ensure the security of your associates' jobs and the future of your company. That should take precedence over outside activities no matter how noble!

I have received valuable advice on outside charitable activities from a couple of my mentors. Our executive vice-president, Marty Ross told me, "Don't ever become the head of anything," because when that top paid professional leaves as they inevitably do from time to time, you end up squarely in the catbird seat. Ewing Kauffman's advice was, "Limit your activities to a total of two in order to be able to continue to give proper focus to the company." My own thought would be to only participate where you feel you can genuinely contribute, not where there is already expertise far beyond your own on a board or other activity.

There can be great joy in working with tax-exempt organizations when and where you can focus for an extended period and really help and feel progress. Best of all, the people you work with will become treasured friends!

### Mining for Diamonds

- Consider outside activities when things are going well with your company.
- Limit your activities to a comfortable number and to a comfortable level within the organization.
- Consider carefully time and potential loss of family time.

*I did not find the world desolate when I entered it and as my ancestors planted for me, so do I plant for my children.*
—The Talmud

*If I am not for myself, who will be?*
*If I am not for others, what am I?*
*If not now, when?*
—Hillel

*You make a living by what you get. You make a life by what you give.*
—Sir Winston Churchill (1874–1965),
British Prime Minister

*You have not lived a perfect day, even though you have earned your money, unless you have done something for someone who will never be able to repay you.*
—Ruth Smeltzer

# Appendix A
## Recommended Readings

Buckingham, Marcus and Coffman, Curt. *First, Break All the Rules* (New York: Simon & Schuster, 1999).

Cohn, Ted, and Considine, Ray. *WAYMISH . . . Why Are You Making It So Hard . . . for me to give you my money?* (1-888-WAYMISH).

Collins, Jim. *Good to Great* (New York: HarperCollins, 2001).

Herzberg, Frederick. "One More Time: How Do You Motivate Employees," *Harvard Business Review* (republished January 2003).

McGregor, Douglas. *The Human Side of Enterprise* (New York: McGraw-Hill/Irwin, 1985).

Mackay, Harvey. *Dig Your Well Before You're Thirsty* (New York: Doubleday, 1997).

Mornell, Pierre. *Hiring Smart* (Berkeley, California: Ten Speed Press, 2003).

Smilor, Ray. *Daring Visionaries: How Entrepreneurs Build Companies, Inspire Allegiance and Create Wealth* (Avon, Massachusetts: Adams Media Corp., 2001).

# Index

Your thoughts, comments, and ideas about this book would be most appreciated. (Sorry, it is not possible to honor requests for personal advice.) Write me at:

> Barnett C. Helzberg, Jr.
> 4520 Main Street
> Suite #1050
> Kansas City, MO 64111

> or

> BHelzberg@aol.com

For information about starting an entrepreneurial mentoring program, write to:

> Helzberg Entrepreneurial
>   Mentoring Program
> 4747 Troost
> Kansas City, MO 64110

> Website: HelzbergMentoring.org